THROUGH THEIR EYES

SHADOWS SPEAK

Edited By Lynsey Evans

First published in Great Britain in 2024 by:

Young Writers
Remus House
Coltsfoot Drive
Peterborough
PE2 9BF
Telephone: 01733 890066
Website: www.youngwriters.co.uk

All Rights Reserved
Book Design by Ashley Janson
© Copyright Contributors 2024
Softback ISBN 978-1-83565-581-8
Printed and bound in the UK by BookPrintingUK
Website: www.bookprintinguk.com
YB0598Z

FOREWORD

Since 1991, here at Young Writers we have celebrated the awesome power of creative writing, especially in young adults, where it can serve as a vital method of expressing strong (and sometimes difficult) emotions, a conduit to develop empathy, and a safe, non-judgemental place to explore one's own place in the world. With every poem we see the effort and thought that each pupil published in this book has put into their work and by creating this anthology we hope to encourage them further with the ultimate goal of sparking a life-long love of writing.

Through Their Eyes challenged young writers to open their minds and pen bold, powerful poems from the points-of-view of any person or concept they could imagine – from celebrities and politicians to animals and inanimate objects, or even just to give us a glimpse of the world as they experience it. The result is this fierce collection of poetry that by turns questions injustice, imagines the innermost thoughts of influential figures or simply has fun.

The nature of the topic means that contentious or controversial figures may have been chosen as the narrators, and as such some poems may contain views or thoughts that, although may represent those of the person being written about, by no means reflect the opinions or feelings of either the author or us here at Young Writers.

We encourage young writers to express themselves and address subjects that matter to them, which sometimes means writing about sensitive or difficult topics. If you have been affected by any issues raised in this book, details on where to find help can be found at *www.youngwriters.co.uk/info/other/contact-lines*

CONTENTS

Ark Academy, Wembley

Paris Mckoy Walker (14)	1
Medina Hylton (14)	2
Munisah Farah (15)	4
Faezeh Pilvar (13)	6
Abdunnur Aquilan (13)	7
Shreyas Pancholi (13)	8
Thacsan Neethirajah (14)	9
Edith Baffour (15)	10
Sohini Chatterjee (12)	11
Andrei Lacatus (13)	12
Ayman Mohamed (11)	13
Ayah Amira Kadem Salem (13)	14
Yusra Abikar (13)	15
Hisham Ahmed (13)	16
Aahan Patel (14)	17

Castle Manor Academy, Haverhill

Ethan Salter (15)	18
Jessie Lee (15)	21
Amelia Turley (15)	22
Anabel Joseph (15)	24

Cove School, Cove

Kiera Knight (13)	25
Lucy Hirst (11)	26
Clara Browne (14)	28
Shreeya Thapa (16)	29
Saisha Vohra (11)	30
Tillie Butler (12)	32
Zoe Thomson (15)	34
Aeris Baldwin (12)	35
Shaniya Steadman (11)	36

Anthony Freeman (12)	37
Cherise Edwards (12)	38

Dartford Science & Technology College, Dartford

Tatenda Mbuse (15)	39
Gihanga De Silva (14)	40
Layla Miller (13)	42
Jessica Coy (14)	44
Chizara Enendu (15)	45
Niamh Woodward (15)	46
Olivia Coppinren (12)	48
Zuri G (14)	50
Krithi Sathish Babu (14)	52
Emma Bowler (12)	53
Kanwara Blackburn (14)	54
Ellie Benning (14)	56
Madison Kenny (13)	57
Emma Langdon (14)	58
Nidhi John (12)	59
Rida Robel (14)	60
Rafa Robel (12)	61
Krissa Kharel (11)	62
Mihika Verma (12)	63
Shannon Bright (11)	64
Hannah Gunasekara (12)	65
Poppy Hathaway (12)	66
Hikmah Lamidi (12)	67
Talia Hagon (14)	68
Harriet Smallcorn (13)	69
Grace-Elizabeth Fatukasi (12)	70
Chanelle Ming (12)	71
Felicia Vuong (11)	72

Linton Village College, Linton

Megan Rush	73
Owen McColl (13)	74
Lilian Corbett (16)	78
Alfie Hill (12)	81
Amélie Phillips (12)	82
Ruvi Razemba (14)	84
Rosa Ison (13)	86
Maddy Glentworth (13)	88
Lily Walpole (13)	90
Isla Westlake (12)	92
Mila Greathead (12)	94
Robyn Stringer (14)	95
Kloe Gonçalves Abbott (13)	96
Jasmine Davies (13)	97
Alba Buxton (11)	98
Phoebe Lattimore (13)	99

Oasis Academy Mayfield, Southampton

Adam Sewell (13)	100
Summer Proctor (16)	102
Emma Stacey (13)	103
Freyja Baker (12)	104
Lucie Wren (13)	106
Teegan Brown (13)	107
Freya Webb	108
Wiktoria Korga (13)	110
Jesse Wolfe	111
Georgina Knight (13)	112
Rupinder Kaur (12)	113

Redmoor Academy, Hinckley

Julia Bortacka (12)	114
Erin Blount (12)	117
Holly Szulz (13)	118
Amber Waite (14)	120
Chloe Barrs (12)	122
Mitchell McCarthy (12)	123
Amelia Snook (12)	124
Jaydon Harrison (14)	125

Lily Robilliard (12)	126
Lewis Matheson (14)	127
Ema Dobrescu (12)	128
Martina Dimitrova (15)	129

St Antony's Roman Catholic School, Urmston

Leila Temperley	130
Matthew Hartley (12)	132
Billy Groves (11)	134
Midas Lee (12)	136
Harry Davenport (12)	137
Daniel Robinson (12)	138
Elaine Regan (13)	139
Luca Thornhill (12)	140
William Haskins (11)	141
Enric Nevin	142
Theo Murray (13)	143
Khaled Bakush (12)	144
Zaijian Garcia Percival (14)	145

The West Grantham CE Secondary Academy, Grantham

Oliver Scrivener (13)	146
Tyler Lane (13)	148
Megan Summers (13)	149
Marion Obi-Brown (13)	150
Brodie Hawkins (12)	151
Isabella Cuttle (13)	152
Shanay Pattison (13)	154
Christina Buts (13)	155
Muhammad Hassan Malik (13)	156
Teliah Evans (12)	158
Ben Smith (12)	159
Olutoni Adeniran (13)	160
Eslija Kampare (13)	161
Tracey Pinto (13)	162
Zoe Zsarko (12)	163
Macorly Dixon (13)	164
Blossom Lou-anne Weatherstone (12)	165
Kaitlyn Jameson (12)	166

Gracie-Sue McGibban (13)	167
Roshan Kandel (13)	168
Abbigail 'Alexis' Gray (13)	169
Amy Taylor (12)	170
Betsy Truman (12)	171
Isabella McClelland (13)	172
Jacob Mcleish (12)	173
Charlie Moras-Isaac (13)	174
Hallie Carter-Smith (13)	175
Matthew Derrick (12)	176
Aaliyah Scothern (13)	177
Daniel Jackson-Keirle (13)	178
Ellis Mason (12)	179
Elizabeth Mojisola Raheem (12)	180

Torquay Boys' Grammar School, Torquay

Ethan Bellamy (12)	181
Thomas Hunt (14)	182
Benjamin Bones (13)	184
Lenny Blakesley (13)	186
Ioannis Petsios (14)	188
Joel Beswetherick Sau (12)	190
Jacob Beringer (12)	192
Ed Dearling (13)	193
Zach Blythe (12)	194
Jacob Bond (13)	195
Tristan West (13)	196
Felix Aram (12)	197
Joseph Forty (13)	198
George De Gennaro (13)	199
Oran Campbell (12)	200
Archie Cole (13)	201
Tom Barber (13)	202

Trafalgar School, Hilsea

Jason Parkin (13)	203
Petal Coates (13)	204
Daisy-Mai Smout (11)	205
Tyler Ravensdale-Marina (14)	206
Kaitlyn Rowley (13)	207
Evie Harding	208

Theo Waters	209
Arrielle Deane (13)	210
Tasfia Uddin (12)	211
Isyra Rogers (12)	212
Zoey Coleman (13)	213
Barney Sheppard (14)	214
Jazmin Robertson (11)	215
Archie Diffey (13)	216
Violet Prior-Sinden (11)	217
Milo Jones (11)	218
Daniel Emmerson (12)	219
Lacey Kemp (14)	220
Justin Harris-Steward (12)	221
Kieron Kemp (11)	222
Carmen Pennell (12)	223
Adedapo Ibiyemi (12)	224
Charlotte Westall (11)	225
Ivie Edafiaga (12)	226

Webster's High School, Kirriemuir

Emily Dick (12)	227
Carla Taylor (12)	228
Eve Beattie (13)	229
Tyler Reid	230
Edward Loftus (12)	231
Ava Phillips (12)	232
Penny Taylor (12)	233
Pippa Burns (12)	234
Millie Aitken (12)	235
Devlin Munro (13)	236
Brooke Coventry (13)	237
Tate Watson (12)	238
Mylie Bogue (12)	239

THE
POEMS

Our Generation

Is it okay to say I'm embarrassed of my generation?
Where knives are being used to take lives, not to cut chives.
Some have to live with the thought of their best friend
Dying right in front of their eyes.

Mental health is real,
Living a teenage life shouldn't be such a struggle,
Social media, bullying and peer pressure,
All lead to teens feeling trapped and alone,
I should be having fun, not having to go out
And worry about getting shot with a gun.

Running away because of mental health,
Leading some to take their own life
Before anybody else gets to,
Watching models on social media,
Wishing to look like them, creating this image in my head
I could never really live.

Is it okay to say I'm embarrassed of my generation?
Because I am.

Paris Mckoy Walker (14)
Ark Academy, Wembley

Part Of Your World

I've got food, I've got money, I've got clothes
I've got water and some soap to clean my head down to my toes
I've got a single mom who tries her best
And a dad who's in my home country, living his best life
They say some black couples don't last
But I want more
I wanna walk in the streets at night and not get shot down
I don't want to be treated like a black dog in a pound
I wanna be part of your world
A world where I am free
A world where there is justice and equality
I don't want my black brothers to be looked at as thugs
Yeah, we are angry, maybe we just need a hug
I wonder why some people look at me like I have a contagious disease
Yeah, I might argue with the white kid who is everything but nice
I'm supposed to take in him calling me an offensive word
Never mind
They automatically assume it's my fault, but they don't know the reason
Oops
I accidentally bumped into the old white lady
Now I'm seen as aggressive
I wanna walk, I wanna talk, I wanna play all day and be okay

I wanna have a lower chance of being killed one day
Where can I be?
Where can I go?
I wanna be part of your world.

Medina Hylton (14)
Ark Academy, Wembley

I Don't Get It

I don't get it,
You say that I have a nice skin colour
But because she's 'too dark',
You say I'm 'dark' too

I don't get it,
You say that I'm very smart
But because she fails her test,
You think I'm going to fail too

I don't get it,
You say that I have a great style
But because she has a better style than me,
You say that my style isn't great

I don't get it,
You say that I'm friendly,
But because she spoke rubbish about others,
You believe that I'm going to speak rubbish as well

I don't get it,
You say that I'm going to make it to sixth form
But because they never made it,
You think I'm not going to make it as well

I don't get it,
You say I do a lot of things right,
But because they made a mistake,
You believe that I'm going to make one too

I don't get it.

Munisah Farah (15)
Ark Academy, Wembley

Locked

I am a prisoner of war, locked amidst the deafening sounds of the missiles,
Locked amidst the decaying corpses that form colossal piles.

I am a prisoner of war, locked amidst the eternal hunger and despair,
Locked amidst the battered buildings that have now fallen, broken; broken beyond repair.

I am a prisoner of war, locked amidst the grim shrieks,
Locked amidst the tears that will forever leak,
Amidst our dear country that now sits hopeless, desolate and bleak.

I am a prisoner of war, locked amidst this petrifying sight,
Filled to the brim with an abundance of fright.

This isn't and will never be alright
We deserve rights, we deserve freedom
We simply need them
Peace we will revive.

We will without a doubt survive.

Faezeh Pilvar (13)
Ark Academy, Wembley

The Letter

Dear family,
I am here to tell you that life in the trenches isn't easy.
My comrades tried to gain the high ground,
But it only resulted in blood.
My comrades, lying on the ground still.
My heart stopped for a second,
Looking at my comrade's body
Tears flowed down my face like a stream.
I grabbed my gun,
And I was ready to fire
However, I felt something in my hands,
And it was covered in blood.
My vision blurred second by second.
And when I opened my eyes, I saw light.
Hands carried me to the top of a cloud.
I felt calm, relaxed and soothed.
Suddenly, I was alerted by a soldier
He said the war was over.
Everyone cheered except for me.
The war was like a gateway to hell,
I hope we never experience this again.

Abdunnur Aquilan (13)
Ark Academy, Wembley

The Wilting Flower

Once, I woke up
And drank tea out of my cup
After that, I looked in the mirror to see my reflection
Then I realised why when someone saw me
They took a big deflection.

One day, I saw a flower
When it saw someone, it seemed to cower
When I saw it, we seemed to have a connection
It looked at me as if it had a confession.

Every day when I looked at it
It seemed to die bit by bit
The next day the flower had disappeared
It probably felt extremely afeared.

It was the last day of school and
I was quietly doing my math
The teacher looked angry and full of wrath
Someone had said that the thief was me
Now the only option I have is to go to thee.

Shreyas Pancholi (13)
Ark Academy, Wembley

Our Ocean Animals

In the ocean's embrace where the waves do play
Lies a world of wonder, a play to sway
Where creatures great and small roam and sway
In harmony with nature each and every day

The dolphins dance with graceful ease
Their clicks and whistles, a symphony of peace
Their playful antics are a joy to see
A testament to the beauty of the sea

The sea turtles swim at a steady pace
Their shell shelter, their home space
They glide and twirl with gentle grace
A symbol of the ocean's gentle embrace

The whales sing with voices deep
Their hunting melodies are a symphony to keep.

Thacsan Neethirajah (14)
Ark Academy, Wembley

Marching To Freedom - By Edith B

Through pain and strife, black souls have fought for a better life.
Injustice faced with unwavering grace, their power and resilience.
From chains of oppression, they broke free, shaping a world where I can be me.
In unity, our voices preach a strong testament.
I, Edith Baffour, pay tribute and cheer to the black heroes who through centuries have been held dear.
I, Edith Baffour, march to the gates of liberty and freedom with my black brothers and sisters beside me.
I, Edith Baffour, will make an impact in the world for the better for my dear black brothers and sisters.
I, Edith Baffour, will make a way for my people.

Edith Baffour (15)
Ark Academy, Wembley

Confused

We are confused.
Why do we get judged just because of how we look?
We are confused.
Why do we have to work five times harder than him,
And he still gets more advantages than us?
We are confused.
Why don't we all have the same role in this life's play?
We are confused.
How many times do we have to fight and march for our rights? Can't we just have them?
We are confused.
Why is our beautiful, mesmerising culture fading away into thin air?
We are confused.
We ask the same questions to ourselves over and over again,
But yet, there is no answer.

Sohini Chatterjee (12)
Ark Academy, Wembley

Prisoner Of War

P atient behind bars
R oaming around
I solated like animals
S tanding between walls
O ur life is beneath, that's where we bet
N ow where do I go?
E venings sad and miserable
R elationships are all gone

O ur life is ruined
F ar as we become

W hat life is this?
A nxious day by day
R eal-world isolation.

Andrei Lacatus (13)
Ark Academy, Wembley

Football

F ootball is the best
O ur favourite sport is football
O ur love for football is passionate
T he Euros or World Cup is the best thing to watch in football
B ecause of football, I am who I am today
A t the lowest point of your life if you need something try football
L ove football forever
L ove playing football with your friends.

Ayman Mohamed (11)
Ark Academy, Wembley

Love And Hate

Love and hate is like pineapple on pizza,
You never really know the truth from your perspective,
Love and hate is like sweet and sour,
They contrast yet need each other.

  L et us think
  O f what we need to
  V erify our feelings
  E specially each other's perspectives.

Ayah Amira Kadem Salem (13)
Ark Academy, Wembley

The World Is Slowly Fading Away

The world is slowly fading away,
Children dying every day,
Wars, genocides, diseases,
Animals losing their homes,
Some going extinct,
Pollution, pollution everywhere,
Hot places becoming colder,
Cold places getting warmer.

Yusra Abikar (13)
Ark Academy, Wembley

What Can We Do?

I fly about, scouting the premises,
My wings caressing the bright blue sky,
When suddenly, my beady pearls spot something
In the distance, where lie some guys.

My jaw drops in fear,
Hoping for me to disappear.

Hisham Ahmed (13)
Ark Academy, Wembley

Heroes

H elp others
E motional connection
R aising new solutions
O verhaul hatred
E scape harm
S aluted for bravery.

Aahan Patel (14)
Ark Academy, Wembley

Can You See Us Now?

S urrender your peace, for no one can know something as rare as this.
U nderstand that this is what I want, not lies that are there to haunt.
P retend to be a girl in this safe yet lonely lost boy's mind space.
P retend to be a girl is the cruel truth, that's seen in my mind's place.
O penly confide in my friends, "Boys can cry," helps me past dead ends.
R enowned and acknowledged for the wrong reason, why can't I be your son?
T hat's not how a lady should behave, drag those words to the grave.

T ake your time and find your pace, that's what they say, when I speak.
H ere I stand with weights for my hands, my life as it seems has been banned.
E veryone turns to look at me, I beam and bask in my glory.

T his is fact, make no mistake, I hold my soul in hearts you can't break.
R ealise this is a new view, the way I look is not an issue.
A nd then men and women fled, your rules are leaving some of us dead.
N ot knowing what may come next on this journey, hold that value firmly,

S ilent voices carry loud minds, leave our past and our guilt behind.
G row our hair or cut it off to make it short, show them that we've lived.
E xpect to have some rough times, the way we live is not to be criminals.
N ever be blamed, for this is not bad, the strength we have they could've had.
D ire words could be armed as weapons, the urge to find out beckons.
E ventually the protests will subside, live our lives full of pride.
R elive the day you spoke out, your true known self shines without a doubt.

P eople help the people, the things they've said to us could be lethal.
E volution has spiralled, our real names we shall always be called.
O de to the many and the few, whose power we never could have known.
P eace among the people who hear, we will keep each other held near.
L onging for the day I'm not scared to be me, I'll be known as 'he'.
E very day is one step closer, soon this anguish will be over.

Surrender your peace for no one can know something as rare as this…

Can you hear us now?

Ethan Salter (15)
Castle Manor Academy, Haverhill

Try In Vain

She, already crowned with gold of day,
I, to do naught but watch in dismay.
To hear the wails from her soul, hear her cries,
Yet with her mouth closed, words fall from her eyes.
Tis hubris to think you'll survive the fall,
Tis good then, that I don't think that at all.
You are no Icarus, you have no wings,
Where I'll go the flowers bloom, the birds sing.
The subject is you, not this folly,
What matters is you, just step down, join me.
All you say is conjecture, I am sure,
Listen, your fate is not to meet the floor,
My argument is this, you're needed here,
There isn't a soul who won't shed a tear.
Your life does not end in this crescendo,
The ball can stop rolling, please don't let go.
The pain you're feeling can be your motive,
Please, I can help you, I am devoted.
Your mind, body and soul are in discord,
I can help, we'll restore them to accord.
Come down from the edge, I am here for you,
Those are... just words.

Jessie Lee (15)
Castle Manor Academy, Haverhill

I Am Death

I am death.
I am light but I am shadow.
I am day but I am night.

Only once a life of many from a being as forever as my eternal youth.
See a soul so broken the pieces slew across many planes of life.

The shards of a being fade in and out from such eternity it spends.
A body slew across a field in which it is seen lain
Amongst the beings of which its ancestors slain.
A being as innocent and holy as an angel's wishing peace alone
The beings of all worlds begging for mercy from me
As I witness God's choice.

God is no saviour as he demands the end of a life
And witnesses the glow of which he created.
Dooming himself to an eternal loop of destruction.

Each being that comes to me witnesses itself begin and end.
It witnesses the pieces bend and break and clip back into place
As if the beginning had never begun.

The beings of the world welcome my light after each shadow.
Each soul sees the light that beckons from my hand
As it echoes to enter each beam of glowing nothingness.

I am eternally bound to the screams of a cycle
Of which no man eternal or celebrated can end.
I welcome souls into new bodies and I tear the old to youth.
I shed the memories of each life back to a blank slate.

I am slumber but I am wake.
I am sunset but I am sunrise.
I am the end but I am the beginning.
I am death, but I am life.

Amelia Turley (15)
Castle Manor Academy, Haverhill

Tangled In Anxiety

I was busy
Not with school, not with work, not with friendship issues
I was busy trying to silence the thoughts inside my head
Wishing I could just stay in bed
I was busy trying to take deep breaths
Exploring the deep, dark depths
I was busy trying not to attract attention from everyone
Still not willing to open up to anyone
I was busy telling myself everything would be alright
Knowing that right there was a lie
I was busy trying to calm my racing heart
The doodles in my book look like creative pieces of art
I was busy lying to people why I can't hang out
Wandering around my room, filled with doubt
I was busy faking my smile
Still struggling for a while
I was busy drowning in my own pain
But you show me that after the rain there's always a rainbow.

Anabel Joseph (15)
Castle Manor Academy, Haverhill

I Never Quite Learnt

Looking around my home, cramped and sad, swarming with despair,
As I rot away in bed with matted, unwashed hair,
Everything felt like a fever dream,
I know he was in love with my pained screams,
Unhealthy I might be, it's easy to see,
But the trauma controls me, never setting me free,
My love is twisted and sick,
But I just can't get out of his grip,
My obsession won't wither,
And my will to live is only a small sliver,
Finally, it's time; my end of the line,
There are no tears left to cry as I finally die,
The suffocation hurt like a burn; the monster who caused this,
I called my love, who was as pretty as a dove,
Cruel like a raven, I'll finally get the love I was craving,
My time has come; my life is done, my blood run,
In the end, I never learnt, but the tables have been turned,
My love and light now took me in the night,
And scarred, my already destroyed body, I'm coming soon,
Time of death 19:25 in the noon.

Kiera Knight (13)
Cove School, Cove

Flee!

People are raging,
The water is dripping.
From the cup of belief,
I'm tired of sipping.

Filled with fear and distress,
I'm hanging on for dear life,
To that thin strand of hope,
That gets stabbed with a knife.

The fire is burning,
The water is cold,
We keep on running,
As I'm growing old.

When can I leave,
This sad, war-torn place?
I shall miss my true home,
But I must run from the chase.

Okay, now it's my turn,
That was a rocky ride,
Not many lived,
Too many died.

So help them now,
The ones that remain,

For unlike us,
Their lives were slain.

So change your perspective,
And imagine their fight,
Bombs, bodies and bones,
It's a horrific sight.

You can't save them all,
Now that part's not fun,
But you could make a difference,
By just saving one.

Lucy Hirst (11)
Cove School, Cove

Free

I wonder what life would be like through their eyes.
But whose eyes are the ones who look to the trees,
They look to the sun, the rivers, the bees.
I wonder how it'd feel to be so free.
You could run through the grass of meadows ahead,
Hear the chirps of the birds after just being fed,
They'd fly so high, twist and turn,
They seem so free, I wish it were me.

How can you imagine what life is like,
Beyond the bars, beyond the streets and the cars?
How will I know if I've ever looked up at the stars?
I want to see what they see when they can dance in the rain,
Have no worries in their mind, there's never any time for pain.
I'll pray and I'll dream, I will get to see it through mine,
But as I wait, I'll watch it through their eyes.
Maybe one day, I'll get to see, what life's really like, to be finally free.
For now, I'll just wish it were me.

Clara Browne (14)
Cove School, Cove

Yours To Judge

I've tried,
"Smile more," they said, and so I did
"Eat less," they said, and so I did
"Show some skin," they said, and so I did
So why? Why when I look and see my face
All I see

I see, 'disgusting', 'pig', 'asking for it'
All I want is happiness,
I've listened,
"Go on Vogue, then they'll listen," they said, "or Elle."
So why when I did and saw myself,
All I saw,

I saw 'little', 'embarrassing', 'useless'
Why am I not enough?
You hide behind a screen while I'm the one
I'm the one breaking, suffocating, dying and so I've tried
I've tried and I'm done
Is this what you wanted?

Shreeya Thapa (16)
Cove School, Cove

My Life In The UK

My life in the UK
Is where I have to say okay
It feels weird
As my dad has grown a beard
This is my life in the UK

I have never seen a zebra
But I have been to Debra
I say hi
While the people eat a pie
Which is coloured like a zebra

Everything is new
Specially the view
The change in money
From paise to penny
For me, everything is new

I can't say bye friends
I can't say hi dents
With me my friend can't walk
With me my friends can't talk
I can't say bye friends

It is a day of sad
As YouTube is on ads
It is my friend's birthday

And it is a Thursday
This is the day of sad

So this is my life in the UK
Where I have to say okay
It feels weird
As my dad has grown a beard
This is my life in the UK.

Saisha Vohra (11)
Cove School, Cove

Winter Through Their Eyes

Winter through their eyes,
Nature's brush paints a landscape,
Silent beauty speaks.

Snowflakes dance and fall,
Blanket the world in white,
Whispers of pure grace.

Bare branches reach out,
Revealing strength in stillness,
Quiet resilience.

Footprints mark the snow,
Trails of memories unfold,
Journeys left behind.

Icy breath exhales,
Frosty air bites, yet revives,
Winter's kiss so cold.

Children's laughter rings,
Building snowmen, forts and dreams,
Joy in frozen land.

Fire crackles bright,
Warmth embraces frozen souls,
Sharing tales of warmth.

Through their eyes I see,
Winter's magic, cold and bold,
A season to cherish.

Tillie Butler (12)
Cove School, Cove

Through Their Eyes

He thinks I'm attention-seeking,
But I'm not.
She thinks I'm not trying,
But trust me I am;
More than you can imagine.
You think I'm faking it,
But I'm not;
I cannot help it.
They don't know what I'm going through,
Inside my head, a volcano erupts.
They just stand and stare,
Laughing and pointing.
It's like they don't care about me.
It's like they ignore my existence.
If you saw it through my eyes you would know,
It's not my fault you don't see the battles I fight.
The torment and torture I go through each day,
Just to express my emotions and tell people how I feel.
Just to feel like I belong,
In this world made for neurotypical people.

Zoe Thomson (15)
Cove School, Cove

Stop The Storm

I am a child on a sinking ship,
I cannot save anyone or pull them ashore,
For my arms are too short, and I am too scared,
I cannot bail out the water,
For I have no bucket, and my hands already ache,
I cannot stop the storm,
I am not an angel,
I am not a god,
You may sit there and think,
But what storm?
And no boat,
And no water!
But this isn't about a storm, a boat, or water,
It's about school,
It's about us students,
I am a child in a school,
I cannot help anyone or their scores,
For my own is sinking, and these lessons are overwhelming,
I cannot stop others' behaviour,
For I have no voice, and it already aches.

Aeris Baldwin (12)
Cove School, Cove

My Superhero Sister

Outside she wears a mask,
Just like a superhero,
But why might you ask?
Sometimes, her social skills are at zero.

Under her mask,
What does she see?
Task after task,
But she wants to be free.

It may look strange to some,
The scrunching of her face,
Or her annoying hum,
But it's never out of place.

At home she feels safe,
So it's time to explode.
No more being brave
She can empty out that load.

I love my little twister, she's my superhero sister.

Shaniya Steadman (11)
Cove School, Cove

The Eyes Of My Cat

When I eat I rejoice
But when I go to my litter tray,
I have a choice
Do I wait for my owner to change it?
Or do I go in and sit?
So when I go in and do my business
I come out slowly so I don't feel dizziness.
Then I go to my owner's bed where I feel warm and cosy
Then I see her hair, so long and wavy.
And then I fall into a deep sleep,
Tired from what happened with my litter tray,
And as they always say, tomorrow is another day.

Anthony Freeman (12)
Cove School, Cove

Why?

Now I wonder, why?
Why do they deny?
Why don't they supply?
For they can't feel our sorrow,
And they have a tomorrow,
They don't even have to seek,
Or work until they reach their peak,
Now I, whose life has been torn for the sake of war, wonder why,
Why is it us who cry?

Cherise Edwards (12)
Cove School, Cove

Silent Sorrows

In the early morn, I wear my smile as a mask,
Hiding my pain behind a facade, it's such a daunting task.
Off to school, I go, with the scent of roses in my hair,
But beneath the surface, I carry a burden, unfair.
My beauty, a metaphor for something pure and bright,
Like a radiant star in the dark shining with all its might.
It contrasts with the pain I hold deep inside,
A juxtaposition of beauty and turmoil, impossible to hide.

Behind closed doors, the weight I carry is heavy,
Tears flow freely, in the silence, unsteady.
Battles rage within a storm that never seems to cease,
A private turmoil, a soul yearning for a release...

In the quiet room, the tears become a river,
Emotions run deep, like a relentless, unyielding quiver.
I fight a battle within, a war no one else can see,
A private struggle, a soul longing to be free.

But amidst the darkness a glimmer of hope starts to shine,
A chance for healing, a path to growth, a light divine,
Through the pain and turmoil, a strength begins to rise,
A soul reborn, ready to embrace the endless skies.

In the morn light, she wakes up with a sigh,
No need for a mask, as her smile reaches the sky.
The battles of yesterday have made her strong and wise,
No more need for pretence, she's found her sunrise.

Tatenda Mbuse (15)
Dartford Science & Technology College, Dartford

It All Starts With...

When I go back to 2010,
On a cold wintery night,
A sixteen-year-old boy left his home,
To think about his future life.

He was young, wild and free,
Who wanted to be an artist in his dreams,
But no one helped him to get on with it,
As they said, "It's not worth it."

Faced with tears, sorrow and depression,
As he faced the ultimate rejection,
No funds and dying from hunger,
His perseverance couldn't last for longer.

His mind was bleach white,
And hardly take a step toward,
But then he thought *just this once*,
And picked himself back forward.

Hard to believe that now I'm a legend,
Receiving love and affection from the world,
Glad that the youth inside me didn't give up,
Which was the greatest beginning of coming forward.

I trusted myself, I loved myself,
Didn't feel lonely as long as I had myself,
Listened to my heart, went at my own pace,
And go what I wanted in my way.

Perhaps I made a mistake yesterday,
But tomorrow, I'll be a bit wiser,
And yesterday me is still me today,
So, be like a phoenix, rising from the embers.

To all the people who are going through the hardships,
Water and treat your wildflower till it blows,
So one day hard work will pay off by itself,
And it all starts with...
Loving yourself.

Gihanga De Silva (14)
Dartford Science & Technology College, Dartford

His Love

Many a year ago,
I lived by the sea,
Close enough to a man,
to know him by name
However, he never looked
and never spoke to me.

I was a child and he was a child
on the land by the sea
But we never met and he never
went anywhere near others
But I always found him near me
I felt a shiver down my spine
whenever he was near

And that is why, long ago
while walking across the sand near the sea
the wind blew cold through my hair
as I felt his presence once again
quiet as he grew closer and closer
till he is close enough to grab me

The demons of Hell are more
warm-hearted than he
my shoes taken from me as if
I will run away as he locks the door

The room bare of anything,
Locked away in misery

But he continues on saying
our love is greater and stronger
than people older than us
of many far wiser than we

And no one, not angels
not demons or humans
can take that away
my beautiful Annabel Lee

My name leaves his lips
as my body freezes at
the way he describes it, I screamed
he came in and became dark
as he walked towards me
I could see it was over
as I was picked up and everything went dark
And as I left, I felt the sound of the sea call to me.

Layla Miller (13)
Dartford Science & Technology College, Dartford

Inside The Mind Of Edgar Alan Poe

My mind is a prison, it's so hard to escape,
My thoughts are disturbing and full of hate,
I just cannot escape this terrible dread.
I miss my wife dearly, oh, Annabel Lee,
Why did you leave me all on my own?
I'm full of demons that won't let me go.

I've fallen into depression and I can't pull myself out,
Childhood trauma, surrounded by death.
Alcohol and drugs are my only escape,
From the reality of life, confusion and fate.
My deepest scars hide the terror inside,
One of the emptiest hearts alive.

I'm tired of being alone, with the unkindness of ravens and a murder of crows.
Torment and sorrow build a nest on my soul,
While the deafening silence and all of the grief,
Make me believe, that life is all 'A dream within a dream'.

My mind is screaming, asking for help,
For someone to save me, as I cannot escape.
My thoughts and fears are swallowing me whole.
Am I scared of death or being buried alive?
Am I crazy or am I just sad?
I'm a slave to my mind and it's out of my control,
"Oh Lord, help my poor soul!"

Jessica Coy (14)
Dartford Science & Technology College, Dartford

Snakes And Songbirds

Through his eyes, he saw beauty, love and potential
A product that could make the crowd go mental
Through her eyes, he was a rich urchin from the Capitol
Thinking he couldn't care less whether she died or not

As both ripened and went through stress
As both lost and gained something
They search for somewhere safe
They planned to run away

He didn't want in
In his eyes, in this tranquil life, he didn't fit in
Because the Capitol is where he wanted to be
Now new thoughts buzz around his head like a bee

His trust became distant
His lies became more proficient
A dark evil in his mind became more persistent

He shot her in the back
He tried covering up his tracks
Thus creating their own private Hunger Games

Through his eyes, she was a step to success
Through her eyes, he was kind and showed her respect
This ending is now one she would expect.

Chizara Enendu (15)
Dartford Science & Technology College, Dartford

Through The Eyes Of A Woman

Times have changed, the world's improved,
You don't have to feel repressed,
Relax at last; feel free to laugh,
You can even wear a dress.

But make sure you have a rape alarm,
Some keys for 'just in case',
'Cause we're a weaker gender,
A fact we must 'embrace'.

So we had to wear a corset,
For the past two hundred years,
And although we can now breathe again,
New problems have appeared.

Wear too little, and you're a s***,
You're simply tempting men,
But wear too much, and you're 'insecure',
And the cycle starts again.

We're like some kind of Barbie,
Dressed up and tossed around,
We have to bend a certain way,
Or else the sight will just astound.

But they're not a primal creature,
Who need instincts to survive,
They can easily learn some boundaries,
And ignore their sexual drive.

Niamh Woodward (15)
Dartford Science & Technology College, Dartford

Harry Potter, See Through Their Eyes, A Night Breaks Through

I sit on the swaying grass, the wind, the sun,
The wind flies through my hair,
Making it light as a feather,
Sadly the sun sets,
The moon breaks through,
The stars shine,
What a beautiful night,
The dreamy sky turns dark blue,
Now it's time to go,
Don't worry, I'll be back soon.

Harry Potter, the boy who lived,
From a deadly curse,
He shall live,
Having a scar on his head,
Connected to the Dark Lord behind a teacher's head,
At the end, Harry Potter dead,
Who Voldemort tried to kill instead,
Harry strong, got up and ran,
Who killed Voldemort,
With a bright light,
That shot out Harry's wand.

See through their eyes, the hardest, the easiest,
See through their eyes, the strict, the soft,

See through their eyes, the bullying, the shine.
See through their eyes, the beauty, the pain,
See through their eyes, the fun, the cruel.

Olivia Coppinren (12)
Dartford Science & Technology College, Dartford

Broken Butterflies

There were butterflies, bright and yellow,
Floating freely and gracefully,
In the pink-hued light, of the evening sky.

Jaddi sent us out to bake some bread,
Beneath my palms, the dough gently spread.
My sister and I danced in synchrony,
There was joy and laughter and harmony.

In her hazel eyes a speck of light,
A mark of hope and forgotten fright…

Big blackbirds made of tin,
Dark and deadly come running in,
A simple song was torn up by a barrage,
Our only home collapsed to ashes.

In a split second,
I saw her hope turn to fear,
In a split second,
Jaddi and my sister are gone.

No longer here.
Now my soul lives wading in tears,
A child like many, orphaned by this war.

When did murder become defence?
When did children become targets?
When did hope become myth?
And why did the war take my family?

Zuri G (14)
Dartford Science & Technology College, Dartford

Undying Hoax

By the ocean's edge,
Where my waves crash and roar,
Let me wash away your sorrows on this shore.
You try to scream, beneath the moon's quarter,
Your pain submerged, as your head breaks my black surface.

My undying presence,
A hoax you embrace -
You reach for my face, yet sandy fingers efface.
Salty tides sting open wounds bitter,
A piece of heaven beckons, yet you choose to suffer.
Patiently you linger, nowhere else better.
Pacing like a ghost along my ebb and flow.

The world ablaze, invisible smoke wraps around your throat
- Transparent to others, but never to me.
Leaning into my embrace, yet stumbling toward the sea.
Dragging scraped and bruised knees, finding solace in me.
Keep walking solemnly,
No refuge so acerbically sweet,
I'll slowly dye you every shade of blue,
On each clandestine meet.

Krithi Sathish Babu (14)
Dartford Science & Technology College, Dartford

Auschwitz

Inside the camp, we all live in fear,
I am forever trying but am never happy here.
There's no escape and no absconding,
and as friends always leave you, there's no point in bonding.
The Germans striking terror into my heart,
they shout and they bellow, they tear you apart.
Families split, loved ones disappear,
there are no happy feelings, only never-ending fear.
At Auschwitz camp, I've lost my brother,
father, friend and have only my mother.
The showers full of gas, the unbearable dining,
how I wish for some joy, for my old life I'm pining.
But like many, my journey through life surely soon will be cut short,
for the fun of Nazis treating murder as sport.
There is never an escape and never any exits,
from concentration camp, the terrifying Auschwitz.

Emma Bowler (12)
Dartford Science & Technology College, Dartford

Shatter

Your sweetness of love,
A mere facade in which,
You hide through a thick charade.

Through your love eyes,
Lay a treacherous lie.

My adore I gave to you,
The nil of what you returned,
Shows a vacuity of your love.

Through your eyes,
I sought to know,
Was your love a pretence?

Your clandestine affair with my own blood,
Exposed by discovery; the truth revealed,
My trust, once strong, is now long gone,
The wretched betrayal, a sharp pain in my heart,
Like a dagger's deadly hand.

Knowing your deception,
Why must I yearn for your love?
My caged mind of false endearments,
Fills my sweet delusions.

Like a feathery fallen petal,
My heart will slowly cripple,
If I persist in clinging to,
This fleeting love as if it,
Were my very lifeblood.

Kanwara Blackburn (14)
Dartford Science & Technology College, Dartford

More Than A Kid Who Had Cancer

People run away
Each and every day
People who don't care
People who won't listen
Treating you as though you don't breathe the same air.

People would come as close as they dare
And turning to stare
"The girl who's faking it!"
Because she didn't lose her hair

"Run away, she will pass it on!"
"Don't get too close, you'll catch it!"
"She's lying anyway."
Little did they know,
Cancer isn't catching,
There are many types of treatment to undergo
It's not my fault I didn't have chemo!

No matter how much
You try and you plead
People may not believe
But, I'm more than just a kid who had cancer.

Ellie Benning (14)
Dartford Science & Technology College, Dartford

In The Shadows, I Live Within

I live in the shadows of the bustling streets,
wrapped in tattered blankets,
with freezing feet,
at night I shiver, with chattering teeth.

My constant quest is finding shelter,
through my weary eyes, I see the world before me,
In the deep summer heat, I swelter,
but I hold onto hope, like whispers in the air

I cherish the smiles and laughter, I see,
for within the hard times, a spirit remains,
I want this world to set me free,
I yearn for a place to belong, to feel accepted.

Each penny I get is not wasted,
extend a helping hand, my story is yet untold,
every day I am judged and dictated,
For in the eyes of a homeless soul, we see,
strength of the world and humanity.

Madison Kenny (13)
Dartford Science & Technology College, Dartford

Echoes Of You: A Poet's View

Stinging tears streaked and stained my face,
I know the scars of us will never be erased.
My mind is left to host an endless war,
Richoceting on the floor,
Too many reminders of us, us, us...
How can I face you anymore?

Even the poets would never allow something like us to be true,
But I'd rewrite every damn one of their books just so they'd include me and you.
Knowing that causes aches to tremor in my body that no one can soothe;
Not even the truth,
Can pull me away from wanting us two.

This is the last,
The most painful part of our past I have yet to unfurl:
It never would have worked out anyway, because I'm just a girl.

And so are you.

Emma Langdon (14)
Dartford Science & Technology College, Dartford

What I'm Called Today

For me, if a word was absent, it
Would be happiness, sounds like
A crime.
It was a lot, I know, going from
Home to home, not knowing what
was fine.
I was touched and threatened,
Crying and frightened, no seriously
Nothing was fine.
Norma Goddard a
New label for me, but it never
Really defined.
During the war, they sent me a far from
Things I wished I liked.
Click, a sound that changed
My life and turned it down to upright
A model, a star, the role required a name
Something that described the very existence of fame
Marilyn Monroe said a shrill voice decayed
And that, ladies and gentlemen,
That's what I'm called today.

Nidhi John (12)
Dartford Science & Technology College, Dartford

Red String Of Fate

Destined with you,
I envision it through my eyes,
Many say it's false,
But I think it's deceiving.

Bright crimson patent from a distance,
Regardless of the time or place,
The blood between two,
Is like the sun and moon.

Every day, I search for you with ambition in my heart,
Afraid, I think you will leave me waiting like wisterias,
Tearing me into pieces.

In my mind, this feels like a grand fairy tale,
But the distance between us is an unknown prophecy.

Thinking about you, whoever you are,
You make my soul's string frail.
I do, to this day, yearn for the day our paths,
Finally start together.

Rida Robel (14)
Dartford Science & Technology College, Dartford

Makes No Sense

I can write random stuff
Like huff and buff
I can do random actions
Like spins and fractions
It makes no sense
Because there is no fence
To cover the sadness
To show the happiness
What I am doing is nonsense
I am weird to write this
Because I don't know what to fizz
All the sentences and all the confusion
Is happening because of my creativeness
I am showing what I am capable of
To write, to do and to make
You are you, and I am me
So we shouldn't change to fit in
Instead, we make no sense, so we stand out
So we can be different to the others
And make a difference to show we
Make no sense.

Rafa Robel (12)
Dartford Science & Technology College, Dartford

All In One Afternoon

The sky cries a little
The sun shows its shiny face
Then the rainbow appears on the hills
Smelling the earthly soil.

Birds glide on the wind
While making no sound,
No one can break the silence
Even after an afternoon workout.

Sunlight, the colour golden
Shining bright like a diamond,
Not even the clouds can hide the brightness
Even when everyone's mood is down.

When the sun plays
Hide-and-seek in the clouds,
Where the folks start their afternoon workouts,
Where the mountains wear a hat of sunset,
While vanishing in the sky,
The horizon and sunset.

Krissa Kharel (11)
Dartford Science & Technology College, Dartford

An Unknown World

In shadows cast, a world unknown,
Through their eyes, perspectives sown.
A tapestry of thoughts unveiled,
Emotions whispered, dreams assailed.

In every gaze, a tale untold,
A symphony of stories manifold.
Walk in shoes not your own,
Feel the echoes, once alone.

Through their eyes, the colours shift,
In a kaleidoscope, emotions drift.
Empathy's dance, a silent grace,
Connecting hearts in shared embraced.

See the world through different skies,
In someone else's point of eyes.
For in diversity, strength resides,
A tapestry of life, where unity abides.

Mihika Verma (12)
Dartford Science & Technology College, Dartford

Through Their Eyes

In distant gazes, stories unfold
Through myriad eyes, a world untold
Each glance a chapter, a unique view

In weary eyes, tales of battles fought
Through sparkling ones, dreams are sought
Eyes of wisdom, etched with time
Speak in silent rhyme

Through their eyes, love finds its way
Reflecting joy in the light of day
In tear-stained orbs, pain resides
A language unspoken, where sorrow hides

Through the window of the soul, we peer
Embracing the essence, drawing near
For tapestry of gaze wide,
A shared humanity, side by side.

Shannon Bright (11)
Dartford Science & Technology College, Dartford

Bullying

The feeling of happiness left my body
As quickly as air leaves my lungs
I feel the tears well up in my eyes
Like someone was knocking a dam down
The laughter and staring around me
Was hitting my body like waves in the ocean
I was drowning
My body shakes with fear as I walk down the hallway
They're looking
The comments getting to my head
Like they were trying to teach me a lesson
They point and shout like I was in a freak show
I was the main act
They tell me it's a joke and they don't mean it
So I guess it's fine, right?

Hannah Gunasekara (12)
Dartford Science & Technology College, Dartford

All In A Golden Afternoon

Lying there,
The sun is all bare,
With the breeze of the air,
Drifting through my hair.

With the glistening of the sun,
I turn to see the birds having fun,
With the sunset up high,
I look to the sky.

Looking at that sunset,
All my dreams were met,
Up in the treetops and down in the crops,
Where the creatures lie and my singing stops.

As I lie back on the sand resting my weary head,
I soon realise it's time for bed,
So this golden afternoon has been the best,
But now I think it's time for rest.

Poppy Hathaway (12)
Dartford Science & Technology College, Dartford

My Journey

I am Malala, a girl with a dream,
To learn, to grow, to be part of a team,
But in my land, the Taliban regime,
Denied me my rights, my hopes, my esteem.

I spoke up, I raised my voice,
For education, for girls, for choice,
To stand tall, to break free,
To be who we are, to be all we can be.

I journeyed to school, with fear in my heart,
But a thirst for knowledge, a passion to start,
A revolution, a change, a spark,
To light up the world, to make a mark.

Hikmah Lamidi (12)
Dartford Science & Technology College, Dartford

Monday

I'm a spectacular lunar newcomer
A fresh start, a blank slate
Growing old with repetitive commentary
From the ones you love and loathe
But it's not my fault you see
It's how you hold yourself as a society
That's the dilemma - dare I say
Don't advertise me more for stating this truth
Oh, but you will, instead of directing the blame
To the working week or how the days are set
I can't complain, my reputation, although infamous
Is due to you.

Talia Hagon (14)
Dartford Science & Technology College, Dartford

Imagine

Imagine a world, free of pain,
No struggle for fame.

Imagine the people and how they struggle,
While you wish for nothing but trouble.

Imagine your meal,
And how it might not appeal.

Imagine yesterday,
When loneliness seemed so far away.

Imagine that when you forget,
They won't forget.

And imagine how one thing you say,
Could ruin your day.

Harriet Smallcorn (13)
Dartford Science & Technology College, Dartford

A Woman Of Colour

As she walks she glides
They look up as she strides
A woman of colour who had been made to suffer
Who has come across many bluffers
They thought she was just a slave
Who had come from a cave
Not knowing she was great
And she would pave our new age
To release the predicted cage
She says, "I am me,
And you should just see."

Grace-Elizabeth Fatukasi (12)
Dartford Science & Technology College, Dartford

Through My Glasses

Through my glasses, I see a world that is far behind me.
When Mercury rotates, there are already 2 months that have gone away.
It was only yesterday that birds were flying high,
And the trees were full of life.
But now they have all gone bare,
So that is why through my glasses I see a world far behind me.

Chanelle Ming (12)
Dartford Science & Technology College, Dartford

You're The Only One Who Sees Me

To the person who saw me through,
Usually, everyone sees past what I am or what I might become,
But when you looked you saw something more.
To them, I am glass, cold and cracked,
But to you, I am water, living and essential.
I have never been seen before,
It scared me.

Felicia Vuong (11)
Dartford Science & Technology College, Dartford

The White Rabbit

As white as snow.
He is the only one who knows
The way around this place.
The twisted tunnels and hopeless holes,
All tangled and knotted like lace.

His watch is as golden as a star.
It ticked in time with his heart.
Until it broke, that day in time.
That day when he broke the bind of time.
You see his clock commanded.
Everywhere in Wonderland.
Its planes, people and palaces.
They all stopped dead, even Alice.
One day they all awoke from their statues.
To find the clock fixed
It said, "Make sure you choose the right one,
Who is the right one you choose."

Megan Rush
Linton Village College, Linton

Elementary

If a raven, that morning, flew over city spires,
It would spy through tendrils of fog below.
Carriages rattling whose horses perspire,
And see the coiled Thames, its ebb and flow.

It would behold old London, rise, stretch and yawn,
Catch a glimpse through a flat's window pane.
Where a gas lamp lights a hawk-like form,
A man pacing a room, twirling a cane.

In his mouth a clay pipe is gripped,
There's a gleam in his eye and steely resolve.
An intercepted letter, in spidery script,
He holds up close; it's a puzzle to solve.

A code lies within; some dancing men,
A semaphore? He ponders and frowns.
He jots down notes with an old fountain pen,
He nods to himself and looks around.

I watch with a smile, this alchemy I've seen,
Each time he finds a new case to pursue.
From languid frustration to sleuth so keen,
As his pale face turns to a warmer hue.

Once his meditations come to an end,
He beckons to me, this adventure to meet.
As soldier, medic, confidant and friend;
Chronicler of his most extraordinary feats.

We consult and confer, excitement unbound
At the tangled plot; we pull on each thread.
Villainy to thwart, a robbery to confound,
A nemesis spinning an enigmatic web.

With a nod, the detective heads for the door,
A light in his eyes and with me in tow.
Like hounds on the scent, as so often before.
We hail a carriage, to the bank we go.

When we arrive, we go straight to work.
"You know my methods, apply them," he said.
With the help of the doorman and a bank clerk,
We prise a loose brick, find darkness ahead.

A tunnel uncovered, from a jeweller's it winds,
Under Threadneedle Street, deep in the ground
Through to the bank vault, where the sleuth finds
A left behind wallet, in red leather bound.

With a glint in his eye, he lifts up the clue,
Holds it before his unwavering stare.
A Latin motto, engraved in dark blue,
Translated as 'Victory for those who dare!'

"They'll come back for this!" he said with a smile.
"The wallet was precious, the crest much revealed."
"They'll dare," he said, "once more with guile,
To return that evening when darkness conceals."

We resolved then to wait and to call for Lestrade,
Whose men soon arrived, to help foil this crime.
That evening, two figures, both panting hard,
Crawled out of the tunnel, all covered in grime.

Then followed a signal, we commenced the attack.
A cane was brandished and a pistol raised.
The criminals were handcuffed tight at the back,
Led away to the Yard crumpled and dazed.

The Inspector approached with a smile on his face
"How on earth did you catch him?" he said to the sleuth.
My friend replied, "When you've eliminated all trace
Of the impossible, whatever is left must be truth."

Back at Baker Street, before a lit fire,
A violin is caressed in soothing tones.
I ponder the remarkable gifts which inspire
The craft of my friend, Mr Sherlock Holmes.

"How did you know?" I exclaim out loud.
"Elementary," he says with a curious look.
In triumph he is poised, neither vain, nor proud.
As for me, it's certainly one for the book!

As night draws in with the distant thunder,
If our raven there, still high in flight,
It would observe a city slouch and slumber,
Unfolding dark secrets into the night.

Owen McColl (13)
Linton Village College, Linton

Elastic: The Teenage Girl's Recollections

With every stardust studding
Along my eyelid's cliffside wires,
With the jagger of zigzagging icicles,
It's all falling, like Cassiopeia
on my lash line.

Like I can still feel you now,
Like you still live rentless, relentless.
In my mind like the monochroma
Marring the white.

Because it's stents to my dents,
Because you are the red to
my blinked-back midnight blue,
Because it's the needle and thread tying
Myself back together after you.

Tracing the arcing of my lineage,
With my fingertips.
I run my nails over the coiling of
Not the curls in my hair, but all over

This broken film reel of me,
Screaming either at or to
My own reflection, inaudibility

Repelled by the iridescence
Of my bathroom mirror.

Littered with lipstick smudges and
Smattered with subjection.
My first kiss, my last kiss,
My red lips and their eclipse.

The sink's covered in me.
It wears my blood.
It wears the curvature that I lack,
My flesh in sunset colours,
Scarlet skies, bones
Chalky white, milky sunrise.
And then those knuckles that
I just can't crack.

This bloodied mess of just body,
Just skeleton, just skin, just scaffolding.
That familiar smell, and the texture,
It lingers like the scalloped gashes
Engraved on my face
From your fingers.

And the sickening thing is, I
Still want it all, still need it all,
Every fragmented piece-
My unheard musings, my hair, your stare -

Every tap dancing whim in
My backlogged heartbeats.

Spinning, stamping,
In my highest heels,
Throwing my shadow at the wall
Only for it to shatter into thousands
Of these silhouette shards,
Beginning to feel like
Scissors, cutting ribbons
Into my satin hands.

Because with the autopilot
Of picking up the soap bar
And with the ease
Of turning the toothpaste cap,

I play that film reel back,
I rewind it till it snaps -
It still plays, it still plays,
It still rings in my ears
Perfectly content, with elastic alacrity,
Even when I run the tap.

Lilian Corbett (16)
Linton Village College, Linton

Brother, Get The Flamer

I'm gonna need a heavy flamer for this heresy
We need a flamer for these heretics
Brother, get the flamer
Brother
Brother
Get the heavy flamer
We only need heavy flamers for this brother
Brother, call in the battle sisters
Brother, I'm injured
Brother, the med box
Brother, we need a heavy flamer
Now Brother
Brother
Brother, I got the heavy flamer
Brother, let's blast this heretic scum
Brother, we did it
Brother, it's the void dragon
Brother, run
Brother, get the flamer
The heavy flamer.

Alfie Hill (12)
Linton Village College, Linton

The Little China Doll

When I first saw her through that glass-paned window,
it felt like love at first sight,
like I was the best one she felt she'd ever know,
but looking back, I'm not sure I was right,

I came from a vintage shop,
here, any perfections were denied,
where we felt like no one would bother to stop,
and have a look inside,

Then she saw me and picked me up,
she begged for me to be bought,
her mum protested as she drank from her cup,
but then her attention was caught,

By my china face and golden locks,
by my quaint little dress,
her face was full of awe and shock,

I suddenly saw the reason why,
I'd seen her before and she started to cry,
we were best friends before a mean bully took me,
and gave me away so that she could never find me,

So she agreed to buy me
and once again I was as happy as could be,
from then on, we felt so joyful and loved each other a lot,

but then the day came when they moved house,
and left me behind to rot

When they finally returned, as I wished they would,
I was dirty and cold and sad,
but now that I no longer sat there alone,
I really felt ever so glad,

"And that," said her mother, "is the story of the Little China Doll."
"So is the story true?"
"No, of course not," she said,
but I was listening and I understood,
so I was made up in her head.

Amélie Phillips (12)
Linton Village College, Linton

They Gave Me A Label

They labelled me as the class clown,
I never asked for this mask.
I don't want to be the centre of attention,
but that's the only way I'll get noticed in class.
My jokes and laughter are the only way I'll get past

Past the whispers and stares,
of peers who only know me through this mask
I'm clear they judge, they must.
But it's not my labels that they should trust.

They labelled me as the troublemaker,
right from the start.
Without a cause, I am in detention to another
all I want is a pause

They labelled me as all sorts surrounding bad.
A rebel, a wild child, a child with no care
did they really think I didn't care?
I have dreams, big ones
but there is a boundary as all I am is the kid labelled with no dreams

A failure is what I labelled myself as,
A class clown, a troublemaker and all labels under what they declared
so let them declare what I am
I took what I was seen as and made them glare

What people see of me is just a thick mask.
There is a person in my class who sees me as more than just a laugh.
They see parts of me, my strength and talent, that I cannot as those parts of me are all blinded by the past,

a past through of labels stuck to me as if I am just art.

Ruvi Razemba (14)
Linton Village College, Linton

Silent Echoes

In the hollows of the soul, a silent scream echoes,
A voice neglected,
prayers search for comfort unanswered.
On a path lost in a maze of uncertainty,
adrift to the journey's end.
To dispel deep distress, unleash possibilities,
trying to amend.

Alone in a crowded room,
each heartbeat a flight in battle,
Trapped in a shadow of immaculate adoration,
Psychological tricks play in the mind,
Seeking liberation from this world of narration,

Neglected wounds whisper beneath a shallow smile,
An unbalanced weight, tipping to denial,
Let them jeer, let them sneer,
their laughter piercing through,
In life's grand play, it's as though there's nothing to say.

In need of reassurance, the achievement of a goal,
The world, a canvas painted in grey's veil,
Seeking a light to show the way.
Nor an action can move the course away.

A drowning soul, reaching for the surface,
To a barren landscape, devoid of purpose?

Time stretches endlessly,
Eternitites search for light in the darkness of the soul.

Where fear abides, a beacon seems to guide,
A strength within, but the urge to flee,
A flicker of resilience, denying the night,
A soul fallen, with open wings attempts the flight.

Rosa Ison (13)
Linton Village College, Linton

Feelings You Don't See, You Won't See

Heartbroken I may be,
But let it be, my heart is still for you.

You left me, I know that,
But know that I'd never leave you.

Far away you're going,
But going changed home.

Home is still home but not,
But not feeling like home isn't right, it's just my mind.

"It's just my mind" that's an excuse,
But excuses make up most of your vocabulary.

I can't help it, why'd you leave?
But why'd you leave? Another phrase I keep coming back to.

Are you proud of it?
But "Are you proud of it?" isn't fair, you're my mum, you wouldn't be.

That's a lie, right?
But, right can sometimes be wrong, you seemed to prove that.

You're right in your eyes,
But your eyes must be looking away from us.

You must need glasses,
But glasses won't change the way you think.

I wish it would, though that's just a dream,
But dreams you said could always come true.

You said that when you used to say goodnight,
But goodnight really meant goodbye, right?

In that case,
Goodnight.
I'll miss you,
But will you miss me?

Maddy Glentworth (13)
Linton Village College, Linton

Tree

I have stood against all weather:
Wind, rain, snow,
My branches give shelter
From the endless storms.

I have seen so much in my three hundred years,
Many herds of cows, deer, horses,
Many flocks of sheep,
Even pheasants and otters too.

Yet all your lives seem insignificant to me,
I have lived for centuries, seeing
All your pointless wars and destruction,
But also love and happiness.
(The human race is so overcomplicated and weird.)

Once, I was worried that I would be cut for timber:
Urbanisation took so many of my friends,
But I stood strong,
Immune to your metal charm.

Until that fateful day,
That one human came my way,
I thought he would just walk by,
But I saw that evil look in his eyes.

It made shivers run from my roots to my leaves.

He raised the axe above his head,
And before I knew it, I was dead.
Sprawled across the sweet-smelling grass.

Lily Walpole (13)
Linton Village College, Linton

Scarecrow

With a purpose of scaring
But a heart of caring
The scarecrow

As lovely as can be
If only you could see
Through his eyes,
He said, "Follow me."

Through the nights he has seen
And all the seasons there have been
Never, has he ever been so keen
But today must mean

With a heart of straw
He never needed more
He only wanted what he saw

With all the sunny days
And winter stays
He can finally see through the summer haze

He has seen everything from
Weddings
Sad endings
And walks to
Serious talks
And much, much, much more

He's never been able to talk
But he always wished he could walk.

Isla Westlake (12)
Linton Village College, Linton

All My Fault

They say I'm as sly as a fox
Yet as ignorant as the human race
It's all my fault
I added lead to gasoline, created GHGs
This caused climate change, don't you see
It's all my fault
The world is suffocating in heat
No one can set it free
It's all my fault
Freon solved a small problem
But created one that is bigger than the hole in the ozone layer
I never wanted it to define me
The one with this legacy
But that's the way it has to be
Always me
Always me
Always me
Thomas Midgley.

Mila Greathead (12)
Linton Village College, Linton

War And Peace

Look around, can't you see?
Hear the voices, hear them plea.
Take a look,
As this, for sure, you won't see in a book.

In war's cruel dance,
Demons will prance.
In trenches deep,
The dead lie asleep.
This is not the way,
Listen closely, hear them pray.
As guns are shot,
The enemy is fought.

Let there be peace,
And may the bombing cease.
May birds fly free,
Far over the sea.
May flowers bloom,
Like sweet perfume.
So let there be peace,
And may the bombing cease.

Robyn Stringer (14)
Linton Village College, Linton

My Mind

My mind is like a roller coaster:
It spins round and round all day.
My mind is like a young child:
It plays with me until the dust of dawn.
My mind is like a race car:
Competing against every trace of thought.
My mind is like a cheetah:
Pouncing at every opportunity that comes.
My mind is like a tree in the wind:
It sways in all directions.
My mind is like a shape-shifter
It never stays as one.

Kloe Gonçalves Abbott (13)
Linton Village College, Linton

Supernova

I am tired now
I am alone
I am the end
I am the ancient sun

Death, destruction, darkness
Life, liberation, light

I am the nuclear beginning
The creator of new

I am radiant darkness, deafeningly silent
I am beautiful rage, furious calm

Everything, nothing
All things, one
Expanding, collapsing
Everywhere, gone.

Jasmine Davies (13)
Linton Village College, Linton

Falling

We all fall
The leaves fall
The trees fall
Even our world falls
While our world may seem perfect, perfect may not be the world
Perfect is a life with honesty, not lies
Love not hate
Equality, not prejudice
But our world is war, disagreement and deception
Soon, society will fall like the leaves in autumn.

Alba Buxton (11)
Linton Village College, Linton

Pickles

Oh pickles: you're simply the best,
You have a crunch and a zingy zest.
You give me a sweet sensation,
Which helped me rest.
Oh pickles, you tickle my tastebuds.
In vinegar and spices, you soak and marinate,
Creating a taste that we all appreciate,
From cucumber to brine,
You make my eyes shine.

Phoebe Lattimore (13)
Linton Village College, Linton

Spring

Days in winter are over
And I'm seeing the trees, the flowers, the plants
They sprout from the ground, they grow and shine
Growing colour leaves and petals
In the spring the wind flies high
The storms the shadows form
They purify the air from the humidity that lasts so long
To prevent a scorching summer
I want to stay near the freshening water
However, I say, "Why don't we watch the trees bloom?
The leaves thriving bright and strong
Can we watch the petals of the flowers bloom?
Everything blooms at some point
So can we watch everything bloom?"

Spring has so many offers
Spring has so many gifts
Spring has so many holidays
Spring has so many opportunities
One of those opportunities
Is to see nature blooming into petals
And leaves and plants forming from the ground
Why don't we watch the trees bloom?
The leaves thriving bright and strong
Can we watch the petals of flowers bloom?

Everything blooms at some point
So can we watch everything bloom?

The summer heats up
The plants burning from the daylight
Running from the daylight
The plants fall to the ground
Rain is needed
Stop the fire from burning
Argh
Why does the nature burn?
Watching the sadness of the blooming leaves
Burning from the daylight
Dying from the daylight

I'll just have to wait till next spring
To watch the trees bloom
The leaves thriving bright and strong
Can we watch the petals of flowers bloom?
Everything blooms at some point
So can we watch
Everything bloom?

Adam Sewell (13)
Oasis Academy Mayfield, Southampton

The Wrong People

"You need help, you're hanging around with the wrong people"
Wrong crowd, wrong naughty kids.
Those words pierce through your skin so quickly,
What was the wrong crowd?
The people who made you feel alive.
No, they're the right people wrong road.
In my eyes those people are just like me.
Those people are broken down and hurt as miserable as me.
They understand because they have been through as much as you
The care system, social workers, abuse, neglect
Led you down the wrong path, the wrong mindset
You just want to feel something so you choose to be 'bad',
Running away from the police, home, stealing from shops
Because you can't even afford clothes to put on your back.
You didn't have the latest clothes
And you haven't eaten since Friday at school.
No one helps the young kids
Nobody stops and thinks they're in trouble,
Or they need help, their mental health is declining, we should help.
No, people just think we are bad kids, they are not normal,
There's something wrong with us.
So, who is the wrong crowd when you have no one else?

Summer Proctor (16)
Oasis Academy Mayfield, Southampton

Family No Longer Together

Through her eyes the world no longer looks so bright.
Her pillow is damp from tears each night.
Longing to hear his voice once more,
To hold him tight, never letting go
As the tides changed, so did life forever.
Who could have imagined a family no longer together?

Now all we have are memories
And pictures of you in a frame
As the sea becomes their enemy
Life would never be the same.

"You can do this, be brave they say,"
But how can she be brave when the wave made his grave
And she's stuck in this trance of never-ending mourning
It breaks her heart when she wakes up
And doesn't see him come morning.

Nature's cruel in all her actions
She uses her beauty as a distraction
From her evil ways
As her morality fades
Along with their joy
As they cry at the loss of their darling little boy.

Emma Stacey (13)
Oasis Academy Mayfield, Southampton

A Dog's Point Of View

Loyal friend, I see,
Humans' hearts forever mine,
A dog's love, divine.

Morning walks, pure bliss,
Nature's beauty, we explore,
Leash guiding our way.

Chasing squirrels, fun,
Endless games, joy untamed,
My spirit unleashed.

Belly rubs, pure bliss,
Head scratches, sweet melodies,
Love flows through your touch.

Food, oh glorious,
Savouring each tasty bite,
Hunger satisfied.

Dreams, wild and free,
Chasing rabbits in my sleep,
Adventures unfold.

Rain pouring outside,
Cosy shelter, by your side,
Peaceful slumber finds.

Hearing your footsteps,
My tail wags, heart leaps with joy,
You're home, my whole world.

Time passes too fast,
But memories forever last,
In your heart, I'll stay.

A dog's life, profound,
Unconditional love found,
Forever faithful.

Freyja Baker (12)
Oasis Academy Mayfield, Southampton

Medieval Times

There I stood, in the valley of roses
Bluebells and jasmine petals gently sway in fancy poses,
There I stood, admiring our crops
Waiting for their harvest and their last water drops,
The plants gently sway in the breeze
Rapidly blooming with ease,

Now it is time to battle
As we grab our swords to protect our cattle,
We fight for our village and our King
So we have no reason not to win,
The weapons we wield
And our armour and shields,

However, sometimes I dream of something more
Than this simple life, I want to open another door,
Maybe the future will be better
Where no one will have to fretter,
Perhaps there will be easier ways to travel
And more secrets to unravel,
But for now, I'm happy in this village of mine
In the medieval times.

Lucie Wren (13)
Oasis Academy Mayfield, Southampton

Poem About School

School, a place of learning and fun,
Where friendships are formed, one by one,
Teachers guiding us on our way,
Helping us grow each and every day,

Books and pencils, desks and chairs,
Learning new things, expanding our cares,
Maths and science, and history too,
So many subjects, so much to do,

Lunch and breaks are times to play,
Running and laughing, enjoying our day,
Art, music, creativity flows,
Expressing ourselves, letting it show,

School may have challenges, that's true,
But together we'll make it through,
Learning and growing, hand in hand,
In this journey, we'll all understand.

Teegan Brown (13)
Oasis Academy Mayfield, Southampton

Save Thy Earth!

I stay going in circles constantly.
No way out.
No way to go as chained, I am.
Not cared for hurting.
No way out.

Aching is all to feel.
For I am not cared for.
And I am dying.
And who I thought loved me.
Indeed, was killing me.

Rubbish surrounds every part.
Global warming is here.
And who I loved.
Did not bother.
To help the aching.
To help Earth.
Who agrees to let them stay.
On the ground, thy made for them.

But the feeling of leaving.
Is close to happening.
But you can help.
Even if it's only a little.

Don't leave rubbish on me.
Try and save me.

For global warming is bad.
Free me from these chains.
The chains that are holding me.
Tighter than ever before.

Freya Webb
Oasis Academy Mayfield, Southampton

New Game

The golden sword trembles in my sweaty hands.
My breathing is shallow as my hair sticks to my face.

It's no use, it'll repeat no matter what I do.

Ripping this blade of justice through their distorted forms for the hundredth time.
The thorny vines around the hilt dig into my hands as my grip tightens.

It's no use, it'll repeat no matter what I do.

I'm doomed to remain trapped in this game of survival.
Only one line of text greets me as I feel my body begin to fail.

Saved file not found. Start new game?

I knew it would be no use, it'll repeat no matter what I do.

Wiktoria Korga (13)
Oasis Academy Mayfield, Southampton

The Flowers Bloom

The flowers bloom
We watched the sun, as the day had just begun.
Our fondest memories were so profound,
The time we have is forever now.

How the clocks tick, how the birds chirp.
How our love grows, how the dandelion blows.

I see your smile far ahead,
Yet, for now, you're put to bed.
As night grows cold, you never grow old.
My dearest friend, I'll be there for you to the end.

As the clock turns to rust,
Our memories are haunted by dust.
The final tick stops.
The wailing of crows, yet no chirping birds in sight.
As a flower's bloom comes to an end,
I lie it flat along my heart,
For now, we are forever apart.

Jesse Wolfe
Oasis Academy Mayfield, Southampton

To Accept And Feel

Roses are red
The sky is oh so blue
To my one love, I am true
To the moon of my stars, I adore

Yet at night, I wonder why
To my sun, I was faithful
I held back and put up a fight
Now, I gaze alone at the moonlight

Still, I am unsure, yet aware
You cannot change the stars, they do that alone
Fate is invisible yet vital
To the stars, I was true, yet now I know they burn up and die

Love is similar
It comes and goes
Yet for me
I am destined to die alone.

Georgina Knight (13)
Oasis Academy Mayfield, Southampton

Do It For You

Stumbling into school,
Feeling all the glares and scowls,
I sat at a table by myself,
I glanced at the piranhas I called
Best friends just days ago,
Giggling at the mere sight of me,
I told myself,
One day, I'll be free,
One day, I'll be happy,
I took a breath and held back tears,
Feeling stuck,
Eventually, I realised my mindset was useless,
Snakes will be snakes,
They barely like each other,
So, I finally changed
And did something for me.

Rupinder Kaur (12)
Oasis Academy Mayfield, Southampton

Rosie, The Rejected Rose

Oh my god,
You would have never guessed,
What happened to me,
Yesterday!

Sorry,
My name is Rosie,
I am a rose,
Yes, you heard me right,
I'm a rose,
This is what can happen to an unwanted rose,
Like me, On Valentine's Day,
Because I am so perfect,
I had to have been given to a girl,
Not.

I was calmy growing,
In this old woman's garden,
Until a young boy, around twelve,
Plucked me out of the dirt,
And held me in his sweaty hands,
"I hope she likes me,"
At first, I was confused,
What did he mean?
But then it hit me,
He was going to give me to his crush!
I thought I could escape from his disgusting, smelly and sweaty hands,

But I was completely wrong,
At school other boys his age,
Crowded around him, asking,
Who he is giving me to,
If I'm all he's got?
Rude.

This massive group of boys,
Followed us around,
Until the boy holding me,
Approached his beautiful blonde-haired girl,
"Hi angel, may I ask, will you be my Valentine?"
He held me close to her,
She rejected him,
"Sorry, I already have a Valentine, I can't have two,"
The boy was heartbroken,
He dropped me and ran away.

Bursting out crying
I was trampled by tons of boys
My poor red petals are still recovering
Here I am
Still stuck
In the school grounds
At 3am
Luckily, yesterday a teacher saw me
Squashed into the concrete
So she picked me up and put me into the dirt

I am slowly recovering from
That traumatising incident
Hopefully, I won't get into more of this Velantine nonsense next year.

Julia Bortacka (12)
Redmoor Academy, Hinckley

I Won't Let You Take Me Down

I fright,
Every night,
My stomach hurts,
How do you have the nerve?

Tear me to pieces,
As I tell you all my secrets,
How could I trust you?
When all you want to do is argue.

You're the one who made it tense,
With your confident steps,
Aren't you scared you'll get caught?
You always do this non-stop.

I'm not sorry for being me,
So just leave me be,
I will spread my wings,
As you're still attached to those strings,
That are pulling you down.

Now I'm in a better place,
Where I can embrace myself,
And I have the bestest friends,
That I love to spend time with,
People I can trust that won't deceive me,
Thank you so much for being with me,
For the highs and lows.

Erin Blount (12)
Redmoor Academy, Hinckley

Untitled

Through their eyes, they see a role model,
Through their eyes, they see a pretty girl,
Through their eyes, they see a kind girl,
Through their eyes, they see a strong man,
Through their eyes, they see a rich or poor house,
Through their eyes, they see a person wanting to be catcalled,
Through their eyes, they see that girls can cry, but boys can't,
Through their eyes, they see that they can do whatever and won't hurt someone's feelings,
Through their eyes, they can do no wrong,
Through their eyes, they can judge people by the way they talk, walk act, or look,
Through their eyes, there is no punishment,
Through their eyes, they can't hurt someone physically and emotionally,
Through their eyes, they see a person who they think is an easy target,
Through their eyes, they see looks and not personality,
Through their eyes, they can see a short-tempered person,
But...
They will never see what happens or what those people think about themselves,
Through their eyes, they will never see how affected those people are by their actions,
Or how they know that some of them could be true,

When rumours go ahead,
Through their eyes, they can see it's funny,
But they don't see that they cry about them,
Or they might not be able to do anything about it,
Or what happens at home,
Through everyone's eyes, they see themselves differently than everyone else,
Through their eyes, they can never see feelings, thoughts,
Or how hurt that person is.

Holly Szulz (13)
Redmoor Academy, Hinckley

Through Their Eyes

Deep in a palace,
Trapped as a princess, fair,
A royal named Alice, the queen's heir,
Books taught balance,
Pure perfection under the royal stare,
Through their eyes, the princess had learned the art,
But through her eyes, she longed to follow her heart.

Far from the crown,
Just beyond a small town,
A common girl, who wasn't proud,
For her status was far lower down,
Her name was also Alice,
Except she was free,
Not locked in a palace,
She was let be.

Though her heart longed to be free,
Free to have money, power and fame,
Free to do whatever she wanted,
For an empty wallet brought her great pain.

Through their eyes,
Both wished to swap,
Their envy of each other would not stop,

Their dream came true,
They indeed did swap,
Now where they want, their happiness does not stop.

Amber Waite (14)
Redmoor Academy, Hinckley

You And Me

The times we spent together won't ever slip my mind,
I'll keep them in my heart forever,
Although sometimes I feel blind,
Which is because I'll see you again never.

Though the memories live on,
My heart still feels empty,
And at night it's the stars I look upon,
As I look for you in the hope you're looking for me.

You'd always be there,
When I'm ill, when I'm sad and when I needed you the most,
So I hope you still are by just floating in the air,
You'll never truly be gone, even if you're a ghost.

So I'll keep my head up high,
When I think of you, it'll be with a smile,
I'll try my best not to cry,
Even though it's been a while...

Chloe Barrs (12)
Redmoor Academy, Hinckley

Through Their Eyes

Through their eyes I am happy,
Through their eyes, I am smiling,
Through their eyes I am alive,
Through their eyes, I am also invisible.

They don't see me crying at night,
They don't see me as depressed,
They don't see me feeling so isolated and deserted,
They don't see the mental pain.

They don't know how it feels when you,
Can't let it all out,
When you can't get rid of the feeling,
No.

If you did, you wouldn't put me through this.
If you did, you'd know the feeling,
If you did, you'd know this is killing,
If you did, you'd know the feeling.

Through their eyes,
I am not here,
"I am fine."

Mitchell McCarthy (12)
Redmoor Academy, Hinckley

Untitled

I'm only a dog,
So I don't use a bog,
My owner loves me a bunch,
And shares her food when she's having a munch.

Lately, it's been going bad,
My owner lost her dad,
But she still gives me lots of hugs,
And I get rid of all the bugs!

It's only getting worse though,
Her social battery is rather low,
But she still loves me the same,
Yet, I can't help but feel to blame.

Sometimes I wonder,
Sometimes I ponder,
If sometimes I act like I'm the monster.

Sometimes I wish, as I eat food from my dish,
I wish I could see what's going on in her head,
And most importantly...
Through her eyes.

Amelia Snook (12)
Redmoor Academy, Hinckley

The Mountain... Or Is It?

The mountain, oh it stood so tall,
Peering down, looking on us all,
As the sun set, the mountain almost smiled,
The snow, how it looked so wild,
As night fell, the mountain stood tall,
Until snow started to crumble,
An avalanche? What could this mean?
Oh, that mountain... it looked so keen.
See the mountain, it put up a fight,
You could even see an orange light,
Oh no, the light is lava, the mountain
Flooded, flares and ash everywhere.
The mountain sat in despair, for there
Was no mountain there... as lava
Started to crumble, the town
Started to rumble, burning up in flames
For poor Pompei was made...

Jaydon Harrison (14)
Redmoor Academy, Hinckley

Untitled

Through their eyes,
We're like a flock of sheep,
That needs to be herded,
Kept under control,
And contained within boundaries.

Through their eyes,
We're just as dangerous,
As a loaded gun,
That could go off any minute.

Through their eyes,
We're like a wildfire,
That could ignite the moment,
Something goes wrong.

Through their eyes,
They think they are making the right decisions,
Looking at the bigger picture…

But if they just tried,
Looking through our eyes,
The picture may change.

Lily Robilliard (12)
Redmoor Academy, Hinckley

A Rabbit's Life

I sit, I sit and wait,
My human is running late,
I've been alone all day,
Playing with a ball of hay,
Hopping around each room,
I wonder if they will be home soon,
I suddenly hear a door,
And footsteps on the floor,
I can't wait to have some fuss,
And some time for just the two of us,
We will play with the snuffle mat,
I am always good at that,
Then I will get a treat,
My favourite things to eat,
My human is my best friend,
I love the time we spend,
May it never end.

Lewis Matheson (14)
Redmoor Academy, Hinckley

Through Their Eyes

Maybe I'll be a ballerina
Ooo, ooo, a teacher,
Or a triple threat called Tina:
Singer, actor and dancer!

Maybe I'll be a whale,
Or shovel the snow,
Not the hail,
But the pay is too low!

Ice cream seller - that's what I'll do,
Or a comedian,
My friends will join in too,
Or I'll paint a chameleon!

You know what,
I won't race,
Cause it's a lot,
I'll stick to being a pencil case!

Ema Dobrescu (12)
Redmoor Academy, Hinckley

Dream

With gazing smiles,
I felt like a hundred miles,
The new elegant styles,
Ran away from the piles.

The sun lingered in July,
To my dream I said goodbye,
The echoes ended and memories died.

In stories, they lie,
I feel so high,
Look at it from the bright spotlight,
We can call it a night.

Doing nothing but daydreaming,
I am just a teen,
What is my life without my dream?

Martina Dimitrova (15)
Redmoor Academy, Hinckley

What It's Like To Be Free

My life is strange and weird
And to be honest, I'd rather disappear,
I want to hide in a hole deeper than ever before
Because if I'm honest, I'm afraid of getting old,
I'm afraid of growing and getting a job of my own.
Growing up is hard but being yourself helps, being fun and free,
It helps being able to be,
Sometimes you can't be you, like when you're at school
When somebody asks, "How are you?"
I smile and say, "Good, you?"
It's strange to be me, I want to flee and be free,
Escape from here and disappear.
To a place far away and be strange, be me and feel so free,
It's strange to be, and not feel like you're free,
It doesn't matter how hard you try
You'll only get an hour to feel as free as a tree,
Swaying in the wind and not having a care
But it only happens for an hour so be aware.
It's strange to look at animals like a maned wolf
And think, *they don't have to pay to live,*
They run around on all fours in the breeze
Feeling as free as can be
But hey, I'll smile every day and say, "I'd rather stay"
But how good it must feel to be as free as a seal,
Swimming about in the deepest seas

Going as deep as you want without needing to breathe,
For a while at least, it must be good to be free.
As free as a fish, a dog, a cat or a bat flying about as high as you want
Without a care in the world
Being alone and free must feel good to be free.
The worries of work, flying away
Because those thoughts are non-existent in an animal brain
They run, fly, glide, swim or sink
They're as free as can be and don't really need to even think.
They're as free as can be if you look at it this way
But the sad thing is you'll never be that free,
You'll never be able to soar up high or swim deep down
Without a worry crossing your mind,
It's strange to think how free they are
But in some ways, they're as free as we are.

Leila Temperley
St Antony's Roman Catholic School, Urmston

The Horror Of World War One

In the cold windy trenches, with my brothers by my side,
The iced wind whistling through my rifle,
Bombs going off all around me and my trench
When the whistle blew, my body shivered!
We were going over the top!

I was as shocked as my team, thousands of bullets went whizzing by my head
My comrades were being slaughtered with enemy fire
Just then, I saw my best friend in pain, in a mortar crater,
Immediately, I called for a medic but it was too late!
More enemy mortars came crashing down
My friend was in bloody shreds, no, not another fallen soul.

My gosh! I've been hit
My arm, blood pouring, I rush to a medic
I do not want to die today!
My eyes could not believe what they were seeing
Medics as far as a lifetime, my heroes in green, positioned at the enemy lines
I ran as fast as I could, over barbed wire, rotting carcasses, of my enemies and comrades, dead on the cold floor of this torturous war.

I've made it!
In the safe arms of the surviving soldiers

Medics treat my wounds
Thank god I'm here
An officer said, "We will stay here tonight."

Matthew Hartley (12)
St Antony's Roman Catholic School, Urmston

Bully, Please

Waking up early in the morning
Feeling, always, so low
Trying not to think about him
When will this feeling ever go?

I quietly shed so many tears
My days, they felt so long
How can I hate school so much?
Please, God, just what am I doing wrong?

I don't like the negative feeling
Why would someone pick on a friend?
Someone, please tell me how
Does this feeling ever end?

Dear Mr Bully, please may I ask
That you don't hurt me anymore
Have compassion to stop the hate
Let me be proud of who I'm thankful for

Take this poem to help you know
You are certainly not alone
Please stand up and speak out
True bravery you will have shown

So, everyone, let's together unite
Bullies, we just don't care
Help out this world, bring people together
And as one, we can make the world fair.

Billy Groves (11)
St Antony's Roman Catholic School, Urmston

Sleepless Nights

As the midnight slowly surely starts,
I was glaring thoughtfully at the radiant stars,
Even though it was a glorious night,
My night dream will not be a fabulous sight,
As I was lying on my bed with wonders,
I was then abruptly interrupted by a terrifying ponder,
Is this all a dream?
However the day today was as smooth as cream,
So I ignored that question and in a blink of an eye, went to sleep.
Creak! Crack! Crook!
I tried to resist but my muscles were fatigued and stuck,
Then in my dismay and horror, my wardrobe opened with a thud!
Two blazing eyes stared at me fiercely with rage,
Just like an animal concealed in a cage,
As the black figure slowly trudged near
I started to tremble in fear,
But nothing happened…
Then I heard a bell ring midnight with a "Wrong."
I figured out that everything is wrong, wrong, wrong.

Midas Lee (12)
St Antony's Roman Catholic School, Urmston

The Inner Thoughts Of A Chair

In the corner, I silently bear,
A chair with thoughts of a secret lair.
I get sat on so people can rest,
Sometimes, while studying, trying their best.

I have wheels to roll around,
Sometimes, making an annoying sound.
From laughter shared to sorrows wept,
In my place, stories are kept.

Wooden whispers, fabric dreams,
I am where solitude gleams.
I've learned a lot over the time,
My favourite thing is I've learned to rhyme.

Many people have sat on me, some heavy, some light,
Some jumping back in a terrible fright.
They think they're crazy when they hear me talk,
Then they realise they'd rather walk.

Harry Davenport (12)
St Antony's Roman Catholic School, Urmston

Who Am I?

I'm mostly black, with patches of white,
I have bright green eyes, which give me incredible sight.

I am the king and I live in my castle,
With three strange humans, that give me no hassle.

I spend my days dreaming, curled up in my bed,
My nose starts to twitch when it's time to be fed.

I scratch and I pounce, I like to have fun,
I'm as quick as lightning, I just love to run.

I love to be cuddled, it makes me purr,
When my humans stroke my velvety fur.

Have you guessed what I could be?
I'm Fozzie the kitten, and you'll never catch me.

Daniel Robinson (12)
St Antony's Roman Catholic School, Urmston

A Team

In a world, differences collide
Bullying rears its ugly head worldwide.
Ethnicity, sexuality, all under attack,
But we won't let them break our spirit, that's a fact!

Peer pressure whispers, trying to sway
But we'll stand strong, not led away.
Social media, a double-edged sword,
Let's use it to spread love.

The future holds promise, a brighter day,
Let's build bridges, not walls of hate!
Embrace diversity, let's celebrate!
Fun is the key, let's laugh and play,
Spread joy and happiness, every day!

Elaine Regan (13)
St Antony's Roman Catholic School, Urmston

Looking After Our Mental Health

Starting year 7 is a scary time,
But it's time to start to climb.
Making new friends,
Learning about new trends.

Write journals and play games,
Achieve your positive aims,
If there are exam stresses,
It will be fine, there will be successes.

If you cannot sleep,
Remember not to sit and weep.
Don't feel alone,
Keep in the zone.

Don't you worry, ask for advice,
The teachers' parents are very nice.
You know your voice matters,
Make sure your head doesn't end up in tatters!

Luca Thornhill (12)
St Antony's Roman Catholic School, Urmston

Ukraine

Innocent people in Ukraine running for their lives,
All that can be heard are helpless cries,
Russia bombing the towns,
All that can be seen are sorrowful frowns,
All that is heard is *boom! Boom!*
Will this end soon?
People fighting for their country,
Spread across Ukraine is poverty,
Why is Russia being so cruel?
Ukraine sitting in a dark depressed pool,
Help! Help! They yelp,
Their hearts beginning to melt.

William Haskins (11)
St Antony's Roman Catholic School, Urmston

The City Lights

As the shroud of darkness
kills the heartless night sky
the city lights shine in line,

As our naked eye can see
our problems fade away
to live another day

As we can observe that we
observe the light that shines;
which makes us fire in the night.

The colours of the night which
saves us from the silvery moonlight
as we can say to ourselves,
Goodnight.
The city lights.

Enric Nevin
St Antony's Roman Catholic School, Urmston

Kurt Cobain

K illed himself
U sing a gun
R ock star
T een Spirit writer

C reator of sound
O ver in the plain
B ox shaped like a heart
A mazing singer
I n the afterlife
N irvana.

Theo Murray (13)
St Antony's Roman Catholic School, Urmston

Hero

'A hero is someone who voluntarily walks into the unknown',
That's what Libyan knight Mustafa did,
Trembling with fear he cut through the Basilisk's chest,
The poison on his arm and cut his hand clean,
The Basilisk trembled on his feet.

Khaled Bakush (12)
St Antony's Roman Catholic School, Urmston

Phone
A haiku

Play, chat, capture, joy,
Tireless scrolls, hiding harsh trolls,
Taking a toll. Off.

Zaijian Garcia Percival (14)
St Antony's Roman Catholic School, Urmston

The Climate Crisis

You know that you're causing it,
And I know that you don't care,
Buildings flooding, people dying,
From here to there, it strikes much fear,

Okay, it's not just your fault,
But still, you give not a care,
Why do you not see the problem?
People's lives not being spared,

Has it occurred to you that,
While you sit back and relax,
Millions die from floods: swept away,
From their homes, on the ground, they lay,

I ask for one thing, I say,
Don't let innocent parents,
Cry in utter dismay, when children,
So young and frail don't live to see another day

So, remember what I've said,
People unaware: clueless,
As others die violently,
It is nothing less than ruthless,

Though I know, you'll do nothing,
For someone random, you met,
So, for the rest of this short life,
Remember what you did to help.

Oliver Scrivener (13)
The West Grantham CE Secondary Academy, Grantham

How Is This Fair?

Freedom fighter
People protector
Religious defender
Always remember

For the people who fought
Not who taught

I will fight
So you're not in fright

You get parades and a month
I get marches and a day
How is this fair?
How do I bear?

I have honour
You have a banner
I'm a WWII soldier
But apparently you're the fighter.

Tyler Lane (13)
The West Grantham CE Secondary Academy, Grantham

Through Her Eyes

As my girls text, I get ready to go,
What to wear, I don't know,
Lashes, fake tan, lipstick and contour,
Is it too much? Should I put on any more?
A nice dress, dark red and low cut,
Should I go, or should I stay put?

As I leave and walk down the path,
A man starts to follow; I want to turn back,
I feel scared and weak as he walks faster,
Should I carry on? Is this a disaster?

I speed up and put my phone to my ear,
My heart beats faster, trembling with fear,
Faster and faster, he's catching up to me,
Should I walk, or should I flee?

I arrive, all eyes on me,
I start to tremble and feel silly,
I just wanted to have fun,
Should I stay, or should I run?

Surrounded by my friends and joy,
I refuse to let my evening be ruined by a boy,
Why are they like this? It's not fair,
Wherever I go, they always stare.

Megan Summers (13)
The West Grantham CE Secondary Academy, Grantham

Racism

I hide.
I hide myself from their judgeful stares.
If I'm seen, nothing more than hurtful words are thrown at me,
Feels like stones being thrown at me.

When I try to talk to someone,
Only harsh glares and insults are all I get,
I'm treated like an outcast,
Almost like I'm not human.

All of them turn their backs on me,
One thing they have in common is that they all say the same thing.
You're dark, I'm light, we can't mix.
You're dark, I'm light, you're not like us.
The same thing repeated, ringing like a bell in my ear,
Constant ringing.

They say they're human, normal,
But why do they say otherwise for me?
Why?

I'm human, I'm human,
I'm normal... Aren't I?

Marion Obi-Brown (13)
The West Grantham CE Secondary Academy, Grantham

A Lost Boy

I was in Africa,
Until I got taken away,
In the midday,
I got handcuffed,
And nearly starved to death on my way,

As I get bashed around,
I feel like a garbage bag,
Swaying around on the dreadful sea
Waiting for them to take me away,
And now it's not the midday,

We arrived, there were three days from when I got taken away,
Ouch!
Is it my time to go?
I hope not,
I want to explore if I ever will,

I got chained up to a heavy rock
Bang, bang I go
And when they shout at me, it disturbs my flow,
Is this fair?
This is now my life but does anybody care?

Brodie Hawkins (12)
The West Grantham CE Secondary Academy, Grantham

I Am A Champion

I sit,
Sitting tying my shoe,
I am a footballer,
Who lives in poverty.

As I wait for food on the table
I starve again,
Hoping I will someday become the best
I sit at my desk wishing that I could eat.

I did it,
I have become a pro,
I will pay her back,
She will eat proper dough.

Why is it so hard?
Why am I hated?
I want to go,
I need to go.

As I pray waiting for my big break,
I have a smile on my face.
I have brought crates,
Nobody should starve.

I wait.
Wait for my name to be recognised.
I turn on the television.
I am a champion.

Isabella Cuttle (13)
The West Grantham CE Secondary Academy, Grantham

Enviromental (Climate Change)

Short and right
Climate change is out of sight
Because of this awful thing
Humans and animals are losing their homes
This isn't right, this isn't right
Because climate change causes ice to fall and break
What if it hurts an animal that goes in the water?
They will get hurt, this isn't fair
Temperature is increasing very fast
This isn't right, it's also not fair to people's homes and buildings
To be flooding and losing their homes
To have nothing to live in
But yet, it still isn't right
And no one can stop this horrible thing from happening!

Shanay Pattison (13)
The West Grantham CE Secondary Academy, Grantham

Animal's Feelings

I saw and felt that again,
They grabbed me and put me in a lab,
I was so anxious that I stood still,
I could not move, I could not see,
But how are we worth it? What bads have we done?
We are alive, as well, just like all of you,
And you are just using us, just like we are all your toys,
How do your cosmetics relate to us?
To our colourful, suffering bodies.
Let's put testing all cosmetics just on you,
But not on us, leave us alone,
And then I opened my eyes, and realised, I was free,
With hope around all my mind,
Hopefully it'll never be again.

Christina Buts (13)
The West Grantham CE Secondary Academy, Grantham

War Through A Soldier's Eyes

Scary terrifying
Haunted house
Fearless soldier
Horror more solid
Dark night
Super nightmare
Gunshots
Being bang
Loudly out
As creepy
As it
Is to
Fear me
Fast runner
Fastest as
You imagine
No one
Can track
The one
And only
Soldier running
Fear them
Gun clicking
Through the
War noisy
Tank shooting

Bombs blowing
Building slamming
To the
Ground aggressively.
As the
War ends
We can
Go away
From this
Axion war
Going back
Going away.

Muhammad Hassan Malik (13)
The West Grantham CE Secondary Academy, Grantham

Through Their Eyes

Through their eyes is an ordinary boy.
But for Christmas not even a toy.
Just a little house for him and his mum.
Not even a day he could call fun.
Day after day she finally gets paid.
With the money you'd give a maid.
Seeing her son sad and heartbroken.
Her closed-up thoughts finally woken.
With her last little penny, she'd buy what he loves.
A small football and football gloves.
He signed up for a club and did very well,
And eventually, he made it on the news,
Now well known as the greatest of all times.
Cristiano Ronaldo!

Teliah Evans (12)
The West Grantham CE Secondary Academy, Grantham

A Tiger's Life

I hunt
I hunt and sleep and play
I protect my parents with pride
The safety of them I keep
Till I hunt again

I hunt
I hunt and sleep and play
There's something over there
Rabbit
Not a second to lose
I'll tear it to pieces

I hunt
I hunt and sleep and play
There's something over there
Poacher
I'll roar and scare it away
Yeah, you better run

Then finally, Mum's home

I jump up and down
I saved us from our town
I roar in your praise, then
I hunt.

Ben Smith (12)
The West Grantham CE Secondary Academy, Grantham

No One Like Me!

Life has a purpose
But I do not get it
Do what you're told
And you won't regret it

Born different ways
Either brother or sister
Skin colour, weight and height
Why do we bother?

See through my eyes
As I'm always rejected
Thought I could have friends
But this leaves me braindead

Always discriminated
I feel so lonely
If I was born different
Would everyone know me?

If I was born different
I bet I would have friends
If I was born different
I bet I would be loved!

Olutoni Adeniran (13)
The West Grantham CE Secondary Academy, Grantham

The Streets

I left
I left and I left for good
I stayed on the streets
Nowhere to sleep

I sang
I sang and sang my heart out
Hoping to get a few pennies
Guitar playing the noise
My fingers hit each string

Then you came
You came and saved my life
You produced my music
I felt relieved

I am thankful
Thankful for where I am
I have fans
I have fans around the world

I wouldn't be here today
If it weren't
For that man
On the streets.

Eslija Kampare (13)
The West Grantham CE Secondary Academy, Grantham

Animal Rights

A nimals deserve to live a good life,
N o one should be treated differently, not even animals.
I magine if this was you in a cage,
M aybe you should think of the environment.
A nimals are friends, not enemies.
L ikewise, animals have rights.

R emember life wouldn't be the same.
I njection getting put in my friends,
G oing one by one.
H ow would you feel if this was you?
T ormented every day,
S eeing this torture.

Tracey Pinto (13)
The West Grantham CE Secondary Academy, Grantham

Through Their Eyes

We are hungry
We are cold
We just really want a home
I'm so sick of hearing
"Go sniff a line."
People don't get it
They won't understand
It makes me feel like I'm going to sink in quicksand
Hearing my dog shiver in the cold
Makes me feel like I'm going to explode
Listening to people chatting on my name
Makes me feel like this is a game
I shouldn't listen to what they say,
But I start to lose it when it starts to rain.

Zoe Zsarko (12)
The West Grantham CE Secondary Academy, Grantham

Untitled

I saw and felt it again.
They grabbed me and put me on a table.
I was so nervous.
I stood still in fear.
Then I felt them stab a needle in me.
I saw them do it to my friends.
After they finished, some of them died.
Some changed colour and some were fine.
When my turn had finished, I changed colour.
It was my friend's turn.
Before they had picked him up, I quickly rushed towards the man.
I jumped up at him and I bit him on the hand.
Now all of us are free.

Macorly Dixon (13)
The West Grantham CE Secondary Academy, Grantham

The Pitiful Penguin

Skating on ice, my penguin crew,
Antarctica's melting, I wish it wasn't true.
Icy homes now feel the heat,
Worried flippers, a frosty beat.

Fishy feasts become a quest,
Ice is melting, not the best.
Puddles forming, an icy surprise
Our chilly world is saying its goodbyes.

But us penguins, we're tough and strong
And this place is where we belong.
With friends in flippers, side by side
In the melting ice, together we glide.

Blossom Lou-anne Weatherstone (12)
The West Grantham CE Secondary Academy, Grantham

Traumatised

Traumatised
Traumatised as I feel ice-cold hands lifting me up
I wonder where I'm being taken to
Will I see the outside world ever again?

I stay put
I have no choice
My body too paralysed to move
My friends are here
Why?
Why is my fur pink and glittery?

I want to run
But I can't
Is this the end?

Why do you do this to me?
Never would I hurt you
So why do you hurt me?

Kaitlyn Jameson (12)
The West Grantham CE Secondary Academy, Grantham

Freedom

I bounce,
I bounce.
Higher I go,
Then I get a sharp pain.

As I woke from my slumber,
I realised I wasn't surrounded by daises.
I had a tranquiliser dart attached to my fur,
Where am I?

I was in a lab,
A testing lab.
I was being injected,
My fur was turning orange.

I decided I didn't want this,
I hopped up and bit their finger.
The test stopped,
Now we are free.

Gracie-Sue McGibban (13)
The West Grantham CE Secondary Academy, Grantham

The Greatest Player

Greatest player!
People say I am the GOAT and the greatest player of all time.
If you count my Ballon d'Ors,
It is eight times that award has been mine.
People might say I am the greatest player of all time
People like me because I have lots of awards
Eg. Ballon d'Or trophies, and Golden Boots
Some people hate me and some people like me
I don't care what people say
I'm just doing what I like to do.

Roshan Kandel (13)
The West Grantham CE Secondary Academy, Grantham

The Struggle Of Homelessness

Through their eyes I was dirty,
Through their eyes I was lazy,
But they know nothing of my past or my present,
To them , I am an animal with a habit of being lazy,
When that is not true,
Every night I sleep on the cold floor,
When you sleep in your bed,
I dream of what I could have,
As you dream of what you already have,
So many people would tell me to get a job,
Well, don't you think I've tried!

Abbigail 'Alexis' Gray (13)
The West Grantham CE Secondary Academy, Grantham

I Am A Swimmer

I have always grown up swimming,
At school no one understood.
They are mostly footballers, basketball players or runners.
I am the only one,
The one and only swimmer.

At my school, we do most sports in PE
But of course, not swimming.
Never swimming!
Most places don't do swimming,
And unless this somehow changes
It will remain that most places don't like us.
Don't like swimmers.

Amy Taylor (12)
The West Grantham CE Secondary Academy, Grantham

Burnt Down

Our leaves swaying in the tranquil wind,
Living a majestic and wonderful life.
When these disgraceful men come chopping us down,
One by one.
Please tell me,
What is more important, our lives or bonfires?
As I watch people walk past me,
Knowing they are waiting to go home,
To a big happy family.
Whilst I'm waiting to be slaughtered,
And watch all my friends go down with me.

Betsy Truman (12)
The West Grantham CE Secondary Academy, Grantham

Seat

On the bus, I sat,
In my seat, I sit,
No rules disobeyed,
No fights to be made,
Alone here I stay,
No games to be played.

Asked to move I have been,
No seats left I can see,
Why move must I?
I shan't move,
I can't.

Why should I go?
This is my seat,
So I tell him no,
Now a fight has been made,
But here still I stay.

Isabella McClelland (13)
The West Grantham CE Secondary Academy, Grantham

The Iceberg

As I lie on the water,
Above a tectonic plate,
All through the night,
I start to lose my shape.

As penguins waddle upon me,
I use my temperature as a fight,
Even though I'm below freezing,
The heat shows its might.

With my pieces flowing around me,
Now always knowing my fate,
Even if I try to stop it,
I know I am terribly late.

Jacob Mcleish (12)
The West Grantham CE Secondary Academy, Grantham

Nadia's Eyes

Hello, my name is Nadia,
My home was beautiful,
But then...

They came and took it all,
The gorgeous forests,
The soft clean covers,
The smell of spices.

Where is my home?

How the once pretty trees,
Are stained with innocent blood.
The sun warns of the day,
The poor screams echo...

Help me!

Charlie Moras-Isaac (13)
The West Grantham CE Secondary Academy, Grantham

Tree

I am never alone,
I look around me and see my friends.
The wind blowing through my leaves,
Day turned to night, back to day.
It is silent,
No birds chirping.
No sun shining.
All I can see is smoke,
All I can feel is ash.
My friends have been burnt down.
Am I next?
I am all alone.

Hallie Carter-Smith (13)
The West Grantham CE Secondary Academy, Grantham

A Poem From A Refugee Called Abdul Javar

My sanity is at its peak

I have lost all I can keep
Many things I have seen

War is bleak and mean
Take me from this race

To see another place
Whether I die or live

My soul shall surely thrive
In heaven or hell
My will you can tell.

Matthew Derrick (12)
The West Grantham CE Secondary Academy, Grantham

Abuse

A buse towards animals.
N ever would I decide to do that to you.
I disagree with the behaviour.
M any animals suffer from it.
A lways rely on us.
L eave them alone, they shouldn't be used as your testing machine.

Aaliyah Scothern (13)
The West Grantham CE Secondary Academy, Grantham

The Homeless

I left my home,
To go to the shop,
I came back and there were spikes,
With everything gone,
Me and my son,
Are nothing but a man and child on the streets,
With nowhere to sleep,
And nothing to eat,
We are also cold.

Daniel Jackson-Keirle (13)
The West Grantham CE Secondary Academy, Grantham

The Drowning Deep

A sunken kingdom,
So deep the colours blinding with the joy of the deep.
Fast as Kraken, a darkness spread
Blinding all who seek its treasure,
Forever surrounded by human eye,
And all because of the land creatures' cry.

Ellis Mason (12)
The West Grantham CE Secondary Academy, Grantham

Climate Change

Climate changes, planet changes
Animals dying
Animals drowning
Plants withering
Trees burning
Seas rising
Houses burning
Weather changing
Accidents happening
Humans dying.

Elizabeth Mojisola Raheem (12)
The West Grantham CE Secondary Academy, Grantham

Environmental Disaster

As I saw my home burn down
I was sad and anxious about what was to come
I smelt the embers burning and heard the crackling of the feared fire
The heat hitting my fur felt like the sun crashing into me
Life has never been worse
This was not the only environmental disaster I had seen
Only a week before this event
I travelled to the sea to have a drink with me and my family
But the water was black and very polluted
Knowing that the water was undrinkable
We travelled another eight miles to drink fresh water
What has our world come to?
Us animals are struggling
We need to stop deforestation and pollution
We are running out of hope
Animals every day are losing their homes
Fires are caused by humans and they are raising the heat on our planet.

Ethan Bellamy (12)
Torquay Boys' Grammar School, Torquay

The Gallows

I am a prisoner.
For an eternity has my stability
Been carved into my cell wall,
By shattered nails sharpened
On the grindstone of insanity.
Waiting, waiting for the day of release.

My tongue greedily snakes its way
Across scores of chipped teeth
And gums long since bled dry,
Expecting the luxury of a meal
That certainly shall never come.
Waiting, waiting for the day of nourishment.

Another prisoner, silent and neighbouring my cell,
He had given in and submitted his soul
To the devilish taxman of sins: the gallows.
They took him away, quiet as an empty house,
I heard nought a scream nor sob.
Waiting, waiting for the day of finality.

The other man was not so voiceless.
His sanity was absent more so even than mine,
And his shrill words would always echo throughout the halls
Contradicting and laughing along with imagined voices.
The maddened laughter upon his withdrawal haunts me still.
Waiting, waiting for the day of death.

As I was taken away, wrapped in chains and bound in cuffs,
I didn't know what noise I would make nor of what volume.
I was brought to the gallows, still in silent contemplation,
Pondering the nature of my certain fate; the pain, the time.
Waiting, waiting for the hour of hanging.

The filthy deck stood upon by ranks of glassy-eyed convicts
Was an image that imprinted its harrowing features onto my mind.
The misty skies surrounded us, the torrential rain soaked us,
All things jostling to witness the butcher's bill.
Waiting. Waiting for the moment of death.

After seeming perpetuity, the floor gave over, not by my weight,
But by the will of that exact thing being the cause of my banishment.
The rope tightens, and strangles me, as I desperately gasp for air
Finally, a resounding crack and all is silent
But the fading march of my gaolers.
No longer does anything have to wait. Not for me.

Thomas Hunt (14)
Torquay Boys' Grammar School, Torquay

The Foxhole

The shells still haunt me,
Trapped in my hole
Like a fox.
Trapped in someone else's war,
The storm of shells blowing over my head,
Shells, shells, and bullets everywhere.

What happened after that?
I cannot seem to remember,
The sound of screams replaces the shells.
Cries of pain and sorrow,
A sensation that can cut deeper than any shrapnel ever could,
And here I am, helpless in my hole.

The wave of camouflage swarming towards our position
Causes even more screams and shells.
Shells and screams,
Now with the additional sound of machine gun fire,
A lawnmower, mowing down the unfortunate ones in front of me,
Brave enough to raise their head,
Brave enough to oppose The Fallschirmjägers.

The sound of marching now accompanies the shells, screams, and bullets.
A never-ending whirlwind of noises in my head,
Our lieutenant calls for retreat

But no one hears the call,
And his body is another one lost in this war,
Another faceless name that will not be remembered.
Darkness,
I am now a mental and physical prisoner,
One of the 'lucky' few to be taken by the enemy.
The rest are lined up and shot,
All pawns in a game of international chess,
Unable to escape their unfair fate.

Now here I am,
In a prison cell
With only my own mad thoughts for company.
And the Private from 2nd Platoon next door,
Now the sound of tanks trundle towards the prison.
No longer a prisoner in my physical state but serving a lifetime sentence in an asylum.

Benjamin Bones (13)
Torquay Boys' Grammar School, Torquay

Thistle

Harshly, the storm clouds blow,
Over where the thistles grow,
A wave of dark moving through the sky,
A foreteller the end may be nigh,
Praying to survive the night,
Wishing to once again see the light,
Wishing to survive the winter.

Eventually, the raging sky dissipates,
It subsides to where the devil waits,
Then the sunshine can defeat the ice,
Freedom from its freezing grasp,
The birds fill the air with their majestic song,
A choir of peace and tranquillity,
Spring brings renewal and hope.

Gradually, the heat intensifies,
Withering rays scorch and sear,
Lesser plants: cower, flinch, succumb,
No defence against the sun's might.
But thistles thrive under the great orb's glow,
Amethyst florets; beacons in a sea of green,
Summer is the giver of radiant splendour.

Slowly, the wind blows again,
Carrying away the last heat of summer,
Returning, the vicious bite of cold,

The last leaves on a nearby oak tree,
Flitter - their long-awaited, swan song.
Cascade towards the now crownless thistle,
When will spring once again arrive?

Lenny Blakesley (13)
Torquay Boys' Grammar School, Torquay

Silence

Silence deafens me,
Silence deafens me,
A faint flicker of light,
A beacon of hope
And a sound

As quiet as a mouse
Yet as elegant as the moon herself.
The particles kiss and the stars dance.
They gather under the veil of darkness.

I am here; love has arrived!
A glorious parade!
Carpets of roses and fluffy balloons of clouds.
Everything for me.

All eyes fixed on my figure,
Succumbed to my charm.
And on my beautiful dress
They would oh so lovingly caress.

They stare at my hair,
So lustrous and long.
Seduced by my cherry-red lips,
So sweet and soft.

I stroll along the river of candles
As it flows past the trees.
I bless them with my touch.
A new life as a gift.

Here is the place I seek,
Hidden in the woods.
Only one sensation felt,
Lust.

A pair of individuals,
Lying down on the grass.
He looked at her the same way
The others gazed at me.

My body vanishes,
It is no more.
Love is now in the air,
For both to explore.

Ioannis Petsios (14)
Torquay Boys' Grammar School, Torquay

Being A Teen

I am a teen
I do what I want
Eating McDonald's
Getting fatter
World ending
I do not care
Parties and all-nighters
Watching thrillers
They are all fighters
Nothing to do
I am all alone
Buying stuff
Taking out a loan
No friends
No one to talk to
No more fun
Looking out my window
Staring at the sun
Nothing to live for
What is the point?
I only have 40 followers
On TikTok
No one likes me
Staying at home
My family wants me to
Buy my own

I am not pulling my weight
I am not making money
So, I found a job
Serving curry
Life is better now
I am friends with the waiters
On Friday night
We grab a bite
Going home all proud
C'mon everyone
Gather around.

Joel Beswetherick Sau (12)
Torquay Boys' Grammar School, Torquay

Guilty

Looking back at what I've done
I've realised that no one's won
Remembering that dreaded night
But I've done the deed and lost the fight

I remember it like yesterday
There sat the safe, as clear as day
I crept through the window frame
And my acts fill me with the greatest shame

But as I crawled across the grass
Lights broke through the night, like cracks in glass
I realised that I'd been found
Frozen with fear, stuck to the ground

And now at last I'm before the court
I hope you'll cut my sentence short
I know I must pay for what I've done
But you see, stealing stuff is just so much fun!

Jacob Beringer (12)
Torquay Boys' Grammar School, Torquay

Racism

R eally, what have I done to deserve this?
A lways being judged like judging a book by its cover
C lamping down on it but does not work
I n crowds there will always be racists
S ometimes I need to ignore it
M any people want to help

I njured but on the inside
N o one knows unless you speak up

F ootball is here to help
O ver time we are stopping this problem
O ccurring over and over again
T here are people to help
B ut it is looking up
A nyone and everyone can help
L et's be proud of who we are
L et's stop this now!

Ed Dearling (13)
Torquay Boys' Grammar School, Torquay

Animal Kingdom

A s I saw my beloved home burn down
N ow I have no home
I do not know where my family and I will sleep
M aybe there will be a tree with space for us
A ll the embers burning up spitting everywhere
L ife has never been worse

K nowing we will be cold and vulnerable tonight
I need to act quickly before matters get even worse
N ow we have nowhere to
G o
D ying, we are with no source of water
O h, why are we animals being tortured once again?
M y cherished kingdom, we... are... dying.

Zach Blythe (12)
Torquay Boys' Grammar School, Torquay

Stick Bug

Crawling across the trees
Hiding when predators are near
Children run around my forest
Picking up sticks and throwing them around
Praying that they don't see me
Now some people have arrived
With large metal objects
They start making a rumbling noise
Heading over to a tree
It goes into a tree and bits of wood fly out
After a minute I hear a crack
And then a boom
The tree had fallen
And now they were heading over to me
I ran down the tree away from the danger
As quick as I could.

Jacob Bond (13)
Torquay Boys' Grammar School, Torquay

King Of The Jungle

I wait and I wait,
Alert and steady,
Ready to pounce,
From the trees,
Like a leopard,

I wait and I wait,
Alert and steady,
As a creature enters my territory,
Not a second to lose,
Within moments it's my dinner,

I wait and I wait,
Alert and steady,
As night falls my senses enhance,
I hear a slight rustling in the bush,
And I leap on it,
Furthermore catching my supper,

I wait and I wait,
No longer alert,
As I slowly doze off...

Tristan West (13)
Torquay Boys' Grammar School, Torquay

The Prisoner

P rison is awful, it is like a burning hell
R egretting all my life decisions, rotting in a cell
I t is horrific, especially the food, everything is cold and tasteless
S o many people talk together but never with me
O nly myself here, me with my thoughts
N ever anything nice, not even the guards
E verything grim here, I am dead inside
R eally having lots of remorse, why did I commit that crime?

Felix Aram (12)
Torquay Boys' Grammar School, Torquay

Hummingbirds

H igh above the ground, I fly
U nder trees and over flowers
M aking noises as I go
M oving with winds that blow me away
I travel across the country
N ectar-eating machine
G oing from place to place at incredible speeds
B eating wings at 80 times per second
I nsects run from my beak
R ed ring around my neck
D evotion runs through my veins
S ymbolising beauty wherever I go.

Joseph Forty (13)
Torquay Boys' Grammar School, Torquay

Prisoner On Death Row

I wait
I dread
The day I shall pay
For all I did wrong
For all I have wounded

I wait
I dread
Only one week left
My sleep is no more
Except a night shivering in fear

I wait
I dread
Time moves slow
Yet my last hours arrive
My last chance to say goodbye

The time has arrived

I walk to my death
The family of victims stare
I sit one last time
My final moments
I'm sorry.

George De Gennaro (13)
Torquay Boys' Grammar School, Torquay

Heroes

H ere I am to help the people who need it.
E veryone is a hero inside, you just need to find it.
R eady to make a difference.
O nly wanting to help.
E ven the best people get angry sometimes.
S ometimes you just have to let it go.

Oran Campbell (12)
Torquay Boys' Grammar School, Torquay

What Am I?

Tail wagger
Joy bringer
Pawprint painter
Food begger
Pat receiver
Love giver
Cosy cuddler
Stick chaser
Shoe destroyer
Human sniffer
Treat chewer
Ear flopper
I am a dog.

Archie Cole (13)
Torquay Boys' Grammar School, Torquay

Prisoner Of War

Mud cleaner
Dish washer
Slop eater
Weight lifter
Gang leader
Wire cutter
Friend protector
Target shooter
I am a prisoner of war.

Tom Barber (13)
Torquay Boys' Grammar School, Torquay

School Sucks!

    S chool: some think it's cool, while others simply drool
    C an such a complex be such complete utter trash?
    H ow about the teachers? What do they think about it?
    O w 'bout da accents? Oo speaks wot 'n' wye?
Y **O** o can' 'ell me ow ta speak mush?
    L ook at that: rooms with too many tables and people.

    S o cramped, yet organised, like an educational prison.
    U kulele lessons and science experiments
    C ontinuous cycles of entering and leaving
    K ids coming in and vandalising the bathrooms
    S chool: some think it's cool, while others simply drool.

Jason Parkin (13)
Trafalgar School, Hilsea

Athlete

You can ask an athlete
To describe the feeling of winning
But only another athlete
Will ever truly understand
What they've been through first-hand
Because you sacrifice your life
To stand on that podium
With that medal
Training five hours a day
With coaches that are cold
And judgemental
No parties at the beach
No joining clubs at school
All work and no play
Every single day
And so
What every athlete looks for
Is that validation
Because it gives you strength
And more motivation
To go back to the gym
The next day
Because a gold medal
Doesn't mean you can go and play.

Petal Coates (13)
Trafalgar School, Hilsea

The Worst Day Of My Life

It started with a sign,
It said the most terrible thing,
'Jews Out!'
We all thought it was a joke,
It wasn't.

The next day I woke up,
And saw the tears in my mother's eyes,
Why is she crying?
She only told me to pack everything,
After, we left home,
And never returned,
We walked through the dirty streets,
We heard guns and screams,
I was terrified.

Luckily my father built a bunker,
Then we were all hidden,
Except my father was stopped and told to pull his trousers down,
He got shot immediately.

Hello, my name is Ari and I am a Jew.

Daisy-Mai Smout (11)
Trafalgar School, Hilsea

Deforestation

D eep in the forest
E very tree slowly dies
F ire engulfing the trees that night
O ceanic seas flood the land
R ed fires blaze and burn
E fficient old men destroying nature
S un burns through the ozone layer
T rees slowly become extinct
A xes swinging, forests disappearing
T itanic destruction of trees
I gnorance of man
O ne big step towards the
N ightmare of extinction.

Tyler Ravensdale-Marina (14)
Trafalgar School, Hilsea

War Life

I wish someone could help me
I can't be at peace in my own thoughts
Not even a safe house to look for
As I explore
Beneath the pile of bricks and stones
I find no toys just blood and bones
My mother is resting with blood on her chest
My father was murdered and laid to rest
I tried not to cry but a tear fell from my eye
Then I heard the shot
I saw it in front of me and fell
My body covered in blood
My bones shattered and falling tears.

Kaitlyn Rowley (13)
Trafalgar School, Hilsea

Covid-19

In 2019, our world got turned upside down
We walked through the streets when there was no sound
A new virus was found
And it slowly drifted to my town

We all got told to stay inside
Otherwise, a lot of us would have died
Boris tried his absolute best
However, everyone was still very stressed

The first lockdown passed
Which surprisingly went very fast
However, it came back stronger than before
Which left us all very bored.

Evie Harding
Trafalgar School, Hilsea

The Old Girl

She's electric with the fans
Like home and seen away
Chants are heard on the other side of town
Super Pompey is playing Mousinho's way

The Fratton End is bouncing
"Blue Army!" gets chanted
PO4 rocks, while the blues
Get all our wishes granted

She's with us through it all,
The good and the bad
Fratton Park is her name
Don't get her sad

Championship: we are on our way!
#PUP

Theo Waters
Trafalgar School, Hilsea

North Sea Nightmare

N erve-wracking waves tower above and crash around me
O blivious to the dangers around, the crew draws in the line
R ush of water sweeps the deck
T ipping the boat with it
H earts pound as we try to avoid being swept overboard

S lipping hands try to hang on but I fall down, down
E vil water engulfs me as my breath slips away
A gasp and a sigh as I awaken from my nightmare.

Arrielle Deane (13)
Trafalgar School, Hilsea

What's Wrong With The World?

The trees are slowly disappearing
Getting chopped down for us
And while they are protesting
We are getting thrown under the bus

But when we cut down the trees
People feel sorry
Because the animals start to flee
People start to worry

Icebergs are starting to fall
Our world is heated up
Polar bears are starting to crawl
While mothers are losing their cubs.

Tasfia Uddin (12)
Trafalgar School, Hilsea

I Am A Victim Of Bullying

Just banter they say, just a "joke,"
Their lies and rudeness make me choke,
You're too heavy, or you're too skinny,
Makes someone's life worse and more dreary,
Let us be us, let us be free,
Dieting and eating, restrictions for physique,
No one should be a victim of your critique,
I am a victim of bullying,
Please leave us be.

Isyra Rogers (12)
Trafalgar School, Hilsea

Not The Body Of Me

The land is barren
Only blood and bones
Sticks and stones
The bodies of my friends
The bodies of my family
The bodies of those who tried to flee
But not the body of me

The bodies of boys
The bodies of girls
The bodies of broken toys
The bodies of birds
The bodies of those who tried to flee
But not the body of me.

Zoey Coleman (13)
Trafalgar School, Hilsea

Hachiroku

I met with new recruits,
in our old, rusty garage.
They all have old cars
in need of mending,
Except for the rich kid
in his dad's Diablo.
Today, we battle the delivery boy
in his AE86 Trueno
named Hachiroku.
He has been drifting along the lanes
since he bought the car in '92.

Barney Sheppard (14)
Trafalgar School, Hilsea

What Am I?

I soar through the sea
Crinkly shell
Jellyfish muncher
Sea carer
Loving parent
Trapped swimmer
Terrified critter
Hoping to see my family
Slowly falling to the bottom
Trying to escape
Seeing my final flashbacks.
What am I?

Answer: I am a sea turtle.

Jazmin Robertson (11)
Trafalgar School, Hilsea

Paul's Grove FC

P icks up the ball on the wing
A rchie at LB
U p the 'grove
L eft-wing
S hoots and scores

G oal!
R eckless tackle
O ver the top of the defence
V ictory
E nergy

F ootball
C lub.

Archie Diffey (13)
Trafalgar School, Hilsea

How The Ocean Makes You

O nly the ocean can make you feel the way you do,
C alm and happy, are the only words you can use,
E ven the breeze can make you feel sleepy,
A nd you only get this feeling when you are near,
N ot only relaxed, all your stress is released.

Violet Prior-Sinden (11)
Trafalgar School, Hilsea

Racism

R acially abused every day,
A thousand people throw rocks every day,
C ouples give me dirty looks every day,
I feel like an outcast every day,
S hoved and shouted at every day,
M illions of roses die around me every day.

Milo Jones (11)
Trafalgar School, Hilsea

The White Room

I always have the same dream:
Where it's just me in a blank white room
A comfy bed
A laptop with my favourite game
No one to distract me
No one to hurt me
No one to bother me or fight me or hate me
No one to tell me everything will be okay
Just me and only me.

Daniel Emmerson (12)
Trafalgar School, Hilsea

The Birthday Disaster

As I wake
I stand in excitement
Put my clothes on
Ready for the day of my life
Just for an empty room
No one
Nothing
Not even a 'happy birthday'
Not even a 'hello'
An empty house I stand in
Alone and scared.

Lacey Kemp (14)
Trafalgar School, Hilsea

The Jewish

J ogging to escape the Nazis,
E ating turnips and cabbage,
W ishing for chocolate,
I run away from my country,
S adness in a station,
H ot and trapped in a boring train cart.

Justin Harris-Steward (12)
Trafalgar School, Hilsea

Untitled

R un away,
H i, are you going to help me?
I am in danger,
N obody is helping me,
O bviously, I'm almost extinct,
S top looking at me, I'm dying, help me!

Kieron Kemp (11)
Trafalgar School, Hilsea

Untitled

Brave whale,
Hungry shark,
Fast fish,
Shy sea otter,
Busy octopus,
Smart jellyfish,
Lonely turtle,
Pretty seahorse,
Cute axolotl,
I am the ocean.

Carmen Pennell (12)
Trafalgar School, Hilsea

A Footballer

Brave warrior,
Goal scorer,
Hard worker,
Fast runner,
Assist maker,
Pleasant person,
Team player,
Respectful teammate,
I am a footballer.

Adedapo Ibiyemi (12)
Trafalgar School, Hilsea

Untitled

Fame seeker,
Charts peeker,
Style icon,
Record breaker.
Hard worker,
Leading lady,
Shady life,
Facing strife,
I am Taylor Swift.

Charlotte Westall (11)
Trafalgar School, Hilsea

Untitled

O ne shiny view,
C alm wavy sounds,
E verlasting brightness,
A lways warm,
N ever loses its beauty.

Ivie Edafiaga (12)
Trafalgar School, Hilsea

Stopping Litter

S topping litter,
T rashing your life.
O pening a new beginning,
P iercing a hole in life.

L ate at night,
I saw a hedgehog stuck.
T hen I got up close,
T o find out that it had been cut.
E nergised, I pick up the hedgehog,
R unning back to the car,
I rushed to the vet.
K **N** eeling down, the vet took the hedgehog,
G etting told that I saved him.

Emily Dick (12)
Webster's High School, Kirriemuir

Cider Pip The Horse

C ider is my name and my owner loves me very much
I f my owner Carla is sad and needs a hug, I have quite the touch
D on't say the word treat around me, I will hear!
E ven when you are not even remotely near
R iding me, you have to have a tight clutch

P roper tight or you can't control me very much
I f you have a bad day and feel a tear
P robably, if you have a treat, I will always be near.

Carla Taylor (12)
Webster's High School, Kirriemuir

Life Of A Funky Fish

I am a fish that lives in a bowl,
That water swooshes, it lights up my soul,
Away I swim, it's been tipped over,
Smack on ceramic, what is this feeling?
Not on ground, not on the ceiling.

Looking in front, horror in my eyes,
Japanese chef, seaweed and rice.

Delicacy served fish and alive,
I have to thank God, but no knife.

Not breathing too well, life of rush,
Lived in a bowl, died in a dish.

Eve Beattie (13)
Webster's High School, Kirriemuir

French Bulldog

Ice is what my owner gives me as water sometimes at 12:00 to stay hydrated in the summer.
As a dog goes past, I bark so I can play with them.
I like my old neighbour's dog. He was an English Bulldog.
He was so cute so I shared my stick with him.
Owner likes to take me on walks down The Den.
I got a new toy and I ripped it apart.
As it is a rope, I can destroy it with my teeth.

Tyler Reid
Webster's High School, Kirriemuir

Can

The can is silver and black
With traces of blue tack
It stays on a beach next to a wrench.
A man sees this can and brings it to his van
He drove off to his workshop where he
Mended it with a pan. *Kabang!* He painted it
Silver and red and put a label on it
Which read 'canned beans'. Next, the man filled
The can with beans and put it in his cupboard.

Edward Loftus (12)
Webster's High School, Kirriemuir

Best Rat Duo

There were two cute, fat rats
Who would like to wear fancy hats
One is called Boo
Who thought he was a cow and went, "Moo!"
The other one is called Peanut
But he has a door to be shut
They both like to eat cheese
Which makes them wheeze
Peanut is a fighter
Who likes to play with lighters.

Ava Phillips (12)
Webster's High School, Kirriemuir

Marlin

M y son is missing,
A nd we'd better find him,
R ound the whooshing sea, he could be anywhere,
L aughter at the happy sea turtles, but we are all upset,
I n the sea, he could be anywhere,
N ight comes, and we have still not found him.

Penny Taylor (12)
Webster's High School, Kirriemuir

Motherhood

M other's work is hard
O ther people might make it look like art
T he kids are so, so loving
H ere are some tips to stop the kids from shoving
E ven a little toy will help the kids play
R ather than the kids getting scored all day.

Pippa Burns (12)
Webster's High School, Kirriemuir

Lottie Fry

As I ride into the arena,
all eyes are on me,
as the light shines,
I'm filled with glee

I'm Lottie Fry, a rider with flair,
me and my horse are one
I inspire you all by bringing elegance into the air,
I ride like the world depends on it.

Millie Aitken (12)
Webster's High School, Kirriemuir

Going To Berlin

Going to Berlin,
With my friend Linn,
We had to stay in an inn.
The bookings were quite thin,
Then we went for a spin,
Now he will win.
But all we got was a tin,
Then we both had a grin.
Stroked our chin,
Then we went back to begin.

Devlin Munro (13)
Webster's High School, Kirriemuir

Purple Cup

Sitting on the bed in tears,
While he is out having beers.
Thinking to myself *love is torture*,
But I feel like I would die without his touch.
Every time he goes, it is like a knife goes right through my soul,
Only he could hurt me like that.

Brooke Coventry (13)
Webster's High School, Kirriemuir

I Fell Out Of A Plane

I fell out of a plane,
Faster than a train,
As scared as a rat,
Getting hit by a bat,
As mindless as a ghost
Eating toast,
And I cried,
As people would say I'd died.

Tate Watson (12)
Webster's High School, Kirriemuir

Anne Boleyn

As I got ready to lose my head
I began to dread
If only I thought to flee
But I loved all the beads
I love Elizabeth, my daughter
I'm sorry for all the slaughter.

Mylie Bogue (12)
Webster's High School, Kirriemuir

YOUNG WRITERS INFORMATION

We hope you have enjoyed reading this book – and that you will continue to in the coming years.

If you're a young writer who enjoys reading and creative writing, or the parent of an enthusiastic poet or story writer, do visit our website **www.youngwriters.co.uk**. Here you will find free competitions, workshops and games, as well as recommended reads, a poetry glossary and our blog. There's lots to keep budding writers motivated to write!

If you would like to order further copies of this book, or any of our other titles, then please give us a call or order via your online account.

Young Writers
Remus House
Coltsfoot Drive
Peterborough
PE2 9BF
(01733) 890066
info@youngwriters.co.uk

Join in the conversation!
Tips, news, giveaways and much more!

- YoungWritersUK
- YoungWritersCW
- youngwriterscw
- youngwriterscw